Name

طَلَعَ الْبَدْرُ عَلَيْنَا
مِنْ ثَنِيْاَتِ الْوَدَاعِ
وَجَبَ الشُّكْرُ عَلَيْنَا
مَا دَعَا لِلهِ دَاعِ

أَيُّهَا الْمَبْعُوْثُ فِيْنَا
جِئْتَ بِالْأَمْرِ الْمُطَاعِ
جِئْتَ شَرَّفْتُ الْمَدِيْنَةَ
مَرْحَباً يَا خَيْرَ دَاعِ

The White Moon rose over us

From the valley of Wadā',

And we owe it to show gratefulness,

For as long as a caller calls out to Allah

O you who were raised amongst us,

Coming with a word to be obeyed,

You have brought to this city nobleness.

Welcome best caller to God's way!

Compiled by Miftaah Scholars and Students.

Printed in the United States of America

CLASS ETIQUETTE

- Write your own detailed notes in your Seerah Workbook. Make your notes reflective of what you learn from each lesson.
- Classes will begin on time, Insha'Allah. Students are requested to try their best to be seated when the instructor is speaking, as not to disturb others by walking in late.
- Please turn off any noise making devices during class time. *This includes the Adhan for prayer time.*
- Please do not speak out of turn while the instructor is speaking, as it may disturb the class.
- We kindly ask students not to record the instructor during class. Recordings will be provided on the Miftaah Institute YouTube channel.
- Students that are younger than 18 must be accompanied by an adult every day.
- Interacting with other students is highly encouraged! However, we kindly remind younger students to limit their interactions with the opposite gender.
- Sessions will run from 9:00 a.m. until 4:00 p.m., and we encourage students to bring snacks and take breaks when necessary.
- Share your GEMs, or "Genuinely Engaging Moments," with other students by writing in your notebook, hanging them on the GEM Tree, and sharing them online.
- Children and babies should not be present while class is in session to avoid disturbing other students.
- Contribute to the class discussion when it is appropriate. Don't interrupt the instructor or another student. Make sure you let other people have a chance to talk.
- Please avoid loud side conversations while the instructor is speaking. You may share any important news with other students outside the lecture hall.
- Although unseen circumstances may occur, students are expected to stay for the entire class session. Please, do not make a habit of leaving while the instructor is talking.
- Show the instructor how much you love this program! Be attentive and active during class by taking notes and asking questions.
- Please try to keep your area as clean as possible in order not to intrude on other students around the table.

TABLE OF CONTENTS

TABLE OF CONTENTS

TABLE OF CONTENTS

TABLE OF CONTENTS

TABLE OF CONTENTS

TABLE OF CONTENTS

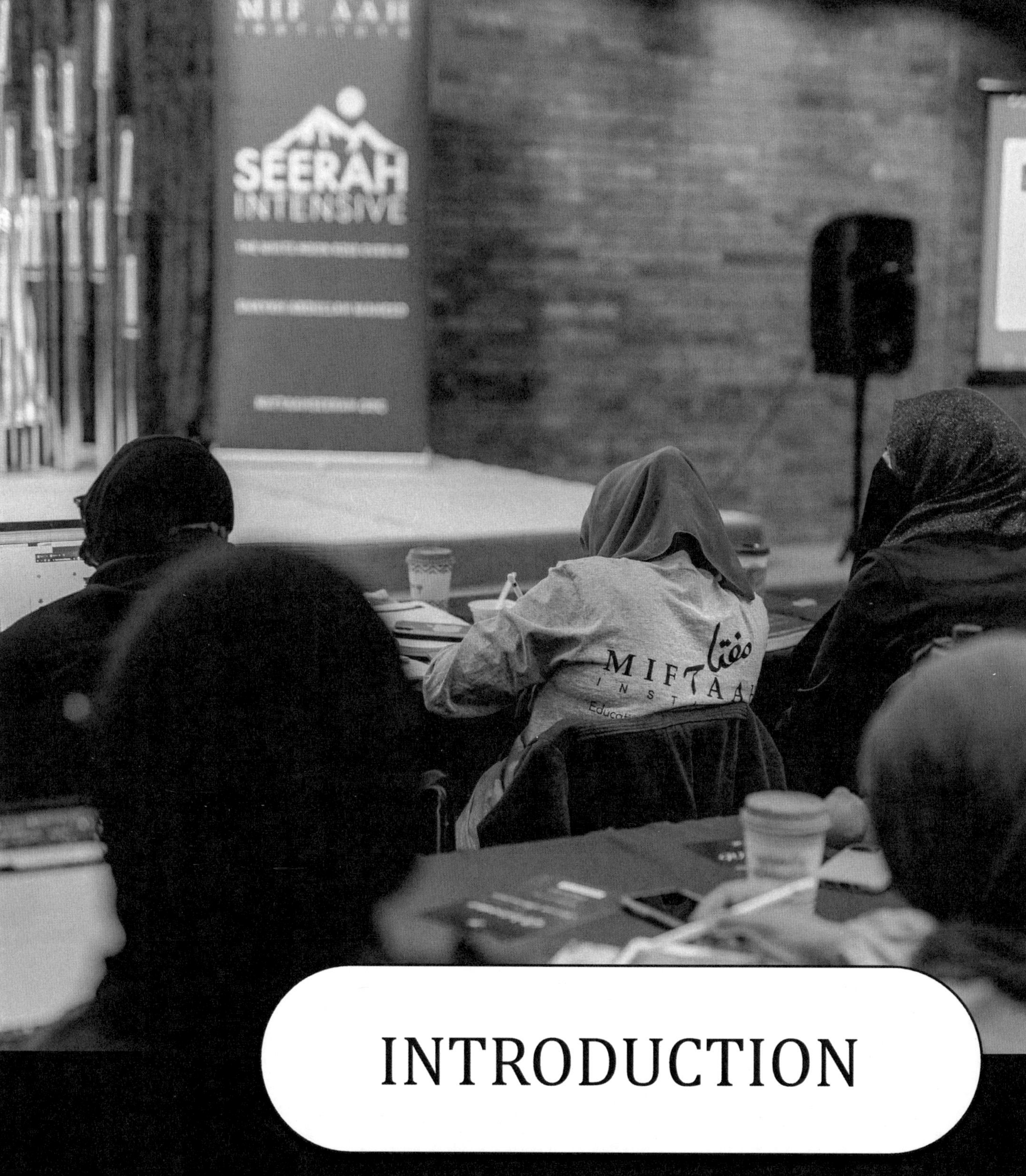

INTRODUCTION

A brief discussion about the virtues of seeking knowledge, as well as an introduction to the subject matter of Seerah and history.

INTRODUCTION

- Prophethood Map: Overview
- Virtues of Seeking Knowledge
- What is the Seerah?
- Seerah Resources
- Intentions for Studying Seerah
- Importance of loving the Prophet ﷺ
- Virtues of Sending Salawat upon the Prophet ﷺ
- Phase Review Questions

Prophethood Map: Overview

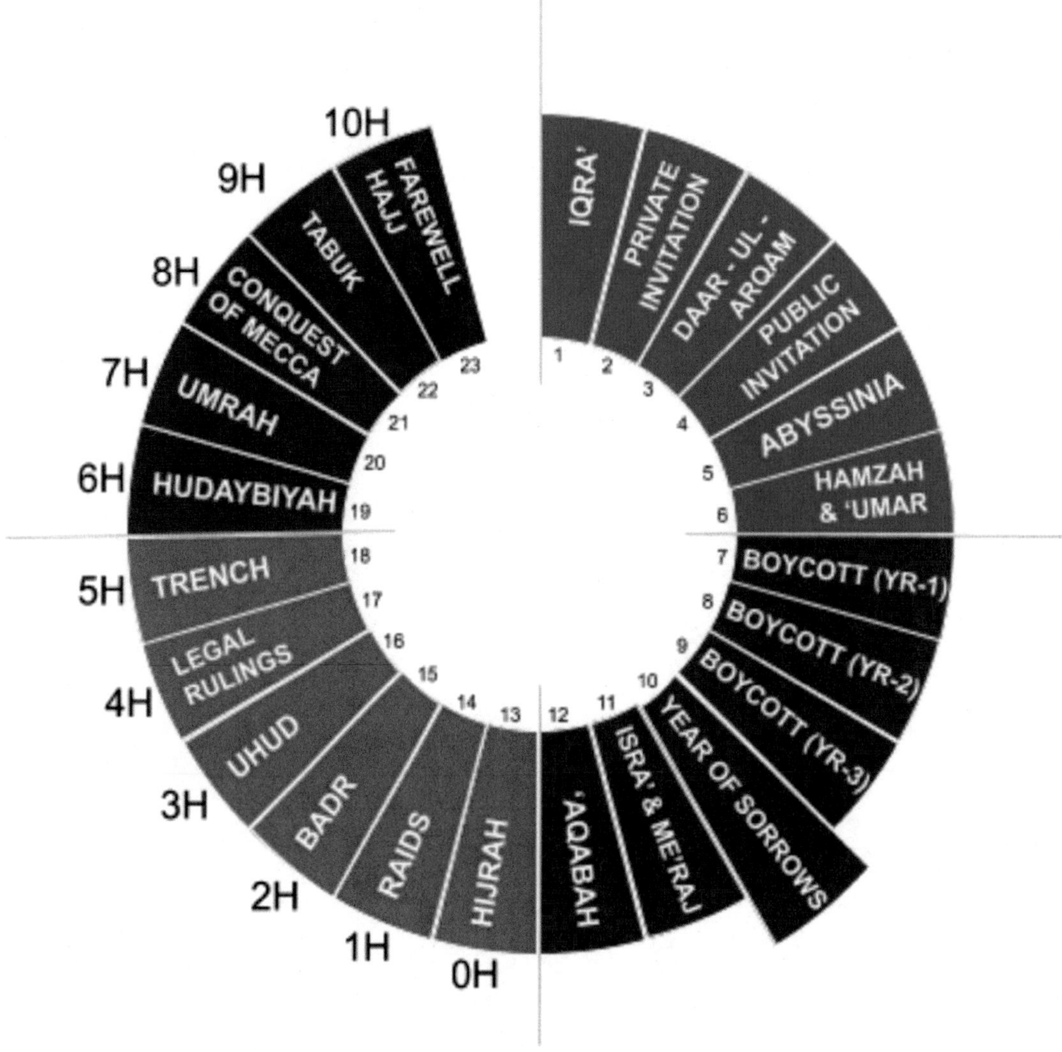

Virtues of Seeking Knowledge

وَقُل رَّبِّ زِدْنِى عِلْمًا

And say, "My lord, increase me in knowledge" [20:114]

قُل هَلْ يَسْتَوِى الَّذِيْنَ يَعْلَمُوْنَ وَ الَّذِيْنَ لَا يَعْلَمُوْنَ

Say, "Are those who know equal to those who do not know?" [39:9]

Why are we studying the Seerah?

مَنْ سَلَكَ طَرِيْقاً يَلْتَمِسُ فِيْهِ عِلْمًا، سَهَّلَ اللّٰهُ لَهُ بِهِ طَرِيْقاً إِلَى الْجَنَّةِ

"Whoever sets out on a path seeking sacred knowledge, Allah will make easy for him the path to Paradise"[Muslim]

What is Seerah?

Seerah

In Arabic the word سيرة comes from the root سار — يسير

Linguistic / Classical Meaning

Early Scholars of Seerah

- Urwa ibn Zubair (d. 92 A.H.)
- Muhammad ibn Ishaq (d. 150 A.H.)
- Imam Muhammad al-Waqidi (d. 207 A.H.)
- Abdul-Malik ibn Hisham (d. 216 A.H.)
- Muhammad Ibn Sa'd (d. 230 A.H.)

Seerah Resources

Primary Sources: Quran and Hadith

Biography based Seerah

- *Siratul Mustafa*- Idrees Kandahlawi
- *The Sealed Nectar*- Safiur Rahman Mubarakpuri
- *Muhammad: His Life Based on the Earliest Sources:* Martin Lings

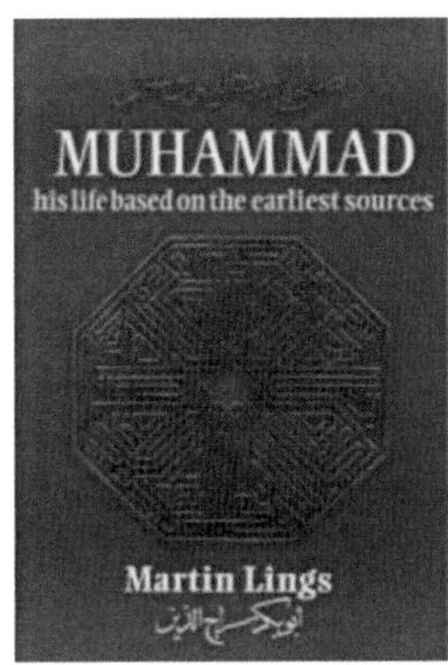

Seerah Resources

Shama'il - Descriptions of the Prophet ﷺ

- Imam Al-Tirmidhi

Dalail Al-Nubuwwa - Proofs of the Prophethood of Muhammad ﷺ

- Al-Bayhaqi

Khasais

Seerah through the lives of the Companions

❤ Speaker's Favorites:

Intentions for Studying Seerah

قُلْ إِن كُنتُمْ تُحِبُّونَ اللَّهَ فَاتَّبِعُونِي

Say, [O Muhammad], "If you should love Allah, then follow me." [3:31]

اَلنَّبِيُّ اَوْلٰى بِالْمُؤْمِنِيْنَ مِنْ اَنْفُسِهِمْ

The Prophet is closer to the believers than what they are to their own lives [33:6]

Ultimate Objective

عَنْ أَنَسِ بْنِ مَالِكٍ قَالَ قَالَ رَسُولُ اللَّهِ ﷺ
لاَ يُؤْمِنُ أَحَدُكُمْ حَتَّى اكُونَ أَحَبَّ إِلَيْهِ مِنْ وَّالِدِهِ وَوَلَدِهِ وَالنَّاسِ أَجْمَعِيْنَ

Anas ibn Malik narrated that the Messenger of Allah ﷺ said: "None of you will truly believe until I am more beloved to him than his children, his father, and all people" [Bukhari]

Importance of Loving the Prophet ﷺ

عَنْ أَنَسِ بْنِ مَالِكٍ، أَنَّ رَجُلاً، سَأَلَ النَّبِيَّ ﷺ مَتَّى السَّاعَةُ يَا رَسُولَ اللَّهِ قَالَ " مَا أَعْدَدْتَ لَهَا " قَالَ مَا أَعْدَدْتُ لَهَا مِنْ كَثِيرِ صَلاَةٍ وَلاَ صَوْمٍ وَلاَ صَدَقَةٍ، وَلَكِنِّي أُحِبُّ اللَّهَ وَرَسُولَهُ. قَالَ " أَنْتَ مَعَ مَنْ أَحْبَبْتَ "

A man asked the Prophet ﷺ "When will the Hour be established O Allah's Messenger ? " The Prophet ﷺ said, "What have you prepared for it?" The man said, " I haven't prepared for it much of prayers or fast or alms, but I love Allah and His Apostle." The Prophet ﷺ said, "You will be with those whom you love." [Bukhari]

INTRODUCTION

Virtues of Sending Salawat upon the Prophet ﷺ

إِنَّ اللهَ وَمَلَائِكَتَهُ يُصَلُّونَ عَلَى النَّبِيِّ يَا أَيُّهَا الَّذِينَ آمَنُوا صَلُّوا عَلَيْهِ وَسَلِّمُوا تَسْلِيمًا

Allah and His angels send blessings on the Prophet: O who believe! Send blessings on him and salute him with all respect [33:56]

قَالَ النَّبِيُّ صَلَّى اللهُ عَلَيْهِ وَسَلَّم، مَنْ صَلَّى عَلَيَّ صَلاَةً صَلَّى اللَّهُ عَلَيْهِ بِهَا عَشْراً

The Prophet ﷺ said: "Whoever prays for Allah's blessings upon me once, will be blessed for it by Allah ten times [Muslim]

جَزَى اللهُ عَنَّا مُحَمَّدًا صَلَّى اللهُ عَلَيْهِ وَسَلَّمَ مَا هُوَ اَهْلُهُ

May Allah SWT reward Muhammad ﷺ on our behalf, such a reward that is due to him [Al-Tabarani]

اَللَّهُمَّ صَلِّ عَلَى مُحَمَّدٍ وَأَزْوَاجِهِ وَذُرِّيَّتِهِ، كَمَا صَلَّيْتَ عَلَى آلِ إِبْرَاهِيمَ، وَبَارِكْ عَلَى مُحَمَّدٍ وَأَزْوَاجِهِ وَذُرِّيَّتِهِ، كَمَا بَارَكْتَ عَلَى آلِ إِبْرَاهِيمَ، إِنَّكَ حَمِيدٌ مَجِيدٌ

O Allah! Send Your Mercy on Muhammad ﷺ and on his wives and his offspring, as You sent Your Mercy on Abraham's family; and send Your Blessings on Muhammad and on his wives and on his offspring, as You sent Your Blessings on Abraham's family, for You are the Most Praiseworthy, the Most Glorious [Sahih al-Bukhari]

Virtues of Saying ﷺ upon hearing the name of the Prophet ﷺ

Phase Review Questions

1. What are some of the virtues of seeking knowledge?

2. What is the literal meaning of *Seerah*?

3. Who are two prominent scholars of Seerah in the early generations?

4. What are the names of three books of Seerah and their authors?

5. What is one virtue of remembering the Prophet ﷺ ?

6. What is your intention for studying Seerah? Mention one goal you have.

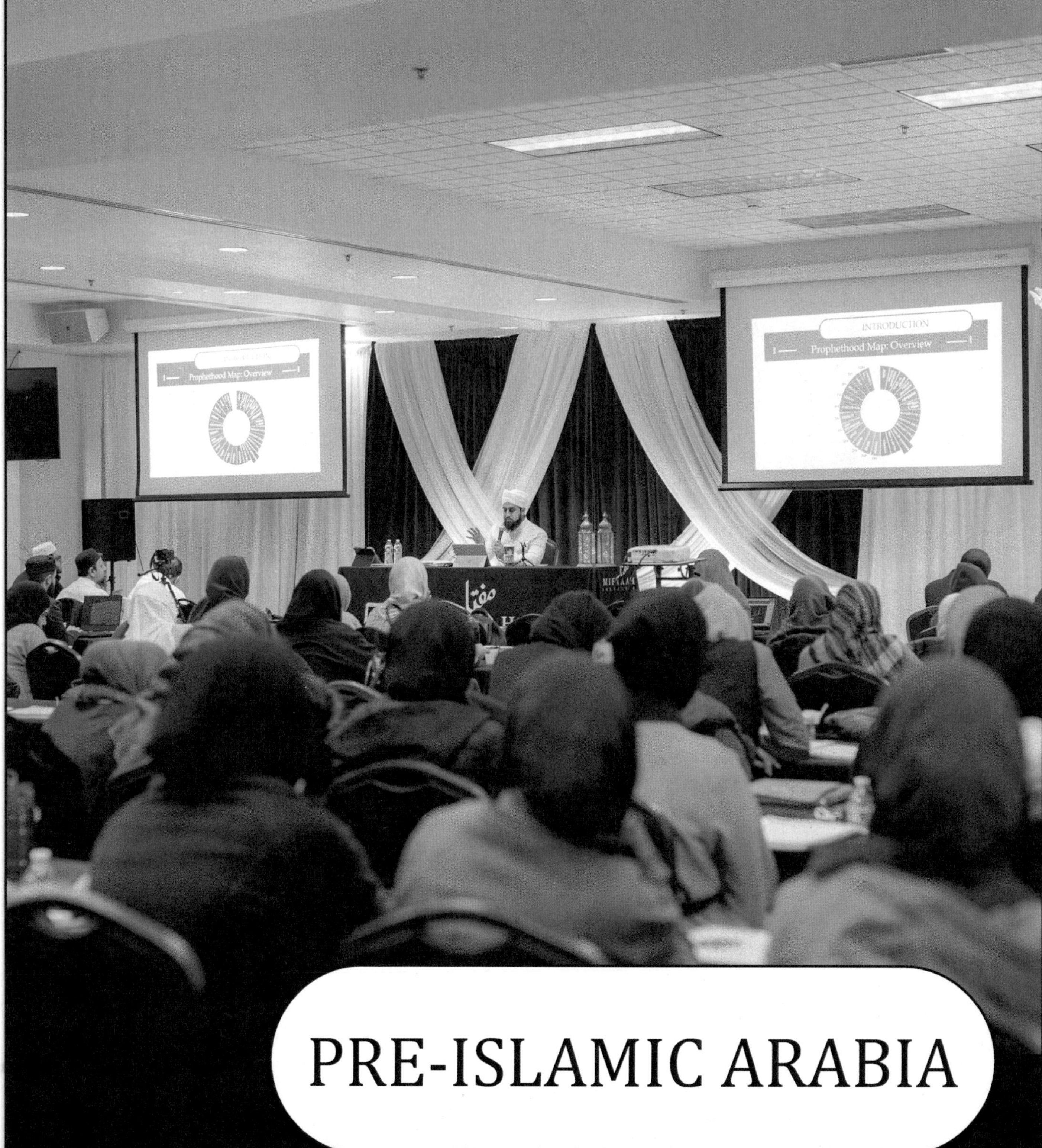

PRE-ISLAMIC ARABIA

A study of the Arabian Peninsula and its inhabitants before the Prophethood of Muhammad W .

PRE-ISLAMIC ARABIA

- Prophet Ibrahim (AS)
- Religion of the Early Arabs
- Three Distinct Groups of Arabs
- Pre-Islamic Traits of the Arabs
- Pre-Islam: Quraysh Tribe and Control of Mecca
- Hashim ibn 'Abd Manaf
- Abdul Muttalib
- Prophet Muhammad's ﷺ Parents
- Prophet Muhammad's ﷺ Lineage
- Phase Review Questions

Prophet Ibrahim ؑ

The Accepted Supplication of Ibrahim ؑ

اَنَا دَعْوَةُ اَبِى اِبْرَاهِيْم

I am the Du'a of my father, Ibrahim [Al-Dhahabi]

There is a very close connection between Prophet Ibrahim (AS) and the Prophet ﷺ despite being far apart historically.

- Prophet Ibrahim (AS) made a du'a when completing the construction of the Ka'bah that a Messenger would be sent to teach these people the true religion of Islam.

وَ اِذْ يَرْفَعُ اِبْرٰهِمُ الْقَوَاعِدَ مِنَ الْبَيْتِ وَ اِسْمٰعِيْلُ ؕ رَبَّنَا تَقَبَّلْ مِنَّا ؕ اِنَّکَ اَنْتَ
السَّمِيْعُ الْعَلِيْمُ ﴿١٢٧﴾ رَبَّنَا وَ اجْعَلْنَا مُسْلِمَيْنِ لَکَ وَ مِنْ ذُرِّيَّتِنَآ اُمَّةً مُّسْلِمَةً لَّکَ
وَ اَرِنَا مَنَاسِكَنَا وَ تُبْ عَلَيْنَا ۚ اِنَّکَ اَنْتَ التَّوَّابُ الرَّحِيْمُ ﴿١٢٨﴾ رَبَّنَا وَ ابْعَثْ فِيْهِمْ
رَسُوْلاً مِّنْهُمْ يَتْلُوْا عَلَيْهِمْ اٰيٰتِکَ وَ يُعَلِّمُهُمُ الْكِتٰبَ وَ الْحِكْمَةَ وَ يُزَكِّيْهِمْ ؕ اِنَّکَ اَنْتَ
الْعَزِيْزُ الْحَكِيْمُ ﴿١٢٩﴾

And [mention] when Ibrahim was raising the foundations of the House and [with him] Isma'il, [saying], "Our Lord, accept from us. Indeed You are the Hearing, the knowing. (127) Our Lord, and make us Muslims [in submission] to You and from our descendants a Muslim nation [in submission] to You. And show us our rites and accept our repentance. Indeed, You are the Accepting of repentance, the Merciful. (128) Our Lord, and send among them a Messenger from themselves who will recite to them Your verses and teach them the Book and wisdom and purify them. Indeed, You are the Exalted in Might, the Wise." (129) [2:127-129]

Prophet Ibrahim ؑ

- Salawat al-Ibrahimiyyah

اَللّٰهُمَّ صَلِّ عَلٰى مُحَمَّدٍ وَّعَلٰى اٰلِ مُحَمَّدٍ كَمَا صَلَّيْتَ عَلٰى اِبْرَاهِيْمَ وَعَلٰى اٰلِ اِبْرَاهِيْمَ اِنَّكَ حَمِيْدٌ مَّجِيْدٌ

اَللّٰهُمَّ بَارِكْ عَلٰى مُحَمَّدٍ وَّعَلٰى اٰلِ مُحَمَّدٍ كَمَا بَارَكْتَ عَلٰى اِبْرَاهِيْمَ وَعَلٰى اٰلِ اِبْرَاهِيْمَ اِنَّكَ حَمِيْدٌ مَّجِيْدٌ

O Allah, bestow Your favor on Muhammad and on the family of Muhammad as You have bestowed Your favor on Ibrahim and on the family of Ibrahim, You are Praiseworthy, Most Glorious. O Allah, bless Muhammad and the family of Muhammad as You have blessed Ibrahim and the family of Ibrahim, You are Praiseworthy, Most Glorious. [Bukhari]

Prophet Ibrahim (AS) was the founder of modern day Mecca.

- Hajar's Migration to Mecca

- Mt. Safa and Mt. Marwa

- Discovery of ZamZam

Prophet Ibrahim ؑ

- Ibrahim (AS) and Ismail (AS) building Ka'bah

- Sacrifice of Ismail (AS)

- All prophets which came after Ibrahim AS were from his lineage.

Similarities between Prophet Ibrahim (AS) and Prophet Muhammad ﷺ

Religions of the Early Arabs

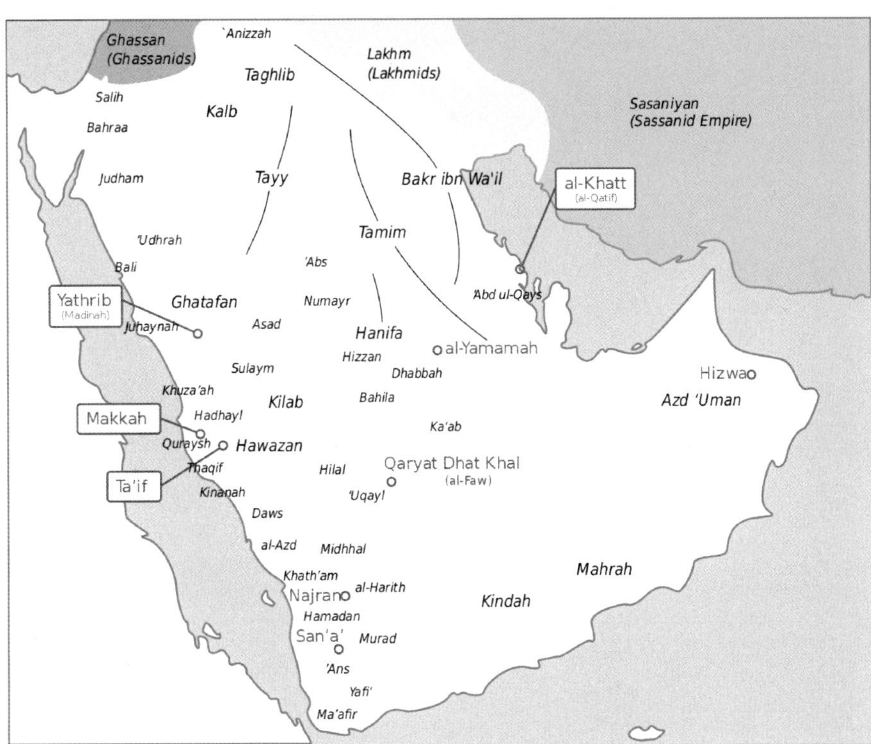

Arabian Polytheism:

Christianity:

Judaism:

Zoroastrianism:

Haneefism:

Three Distinct Groups of Arabs

The Perished Arabs: Descendants of Nuh (نوحٌ) — A'ad (عاد) and Thamud (ثمود)

The Pure Arabs: Qahtanian Arabs (Yemen)

The Arabized Arabs: Lineage of Ismail

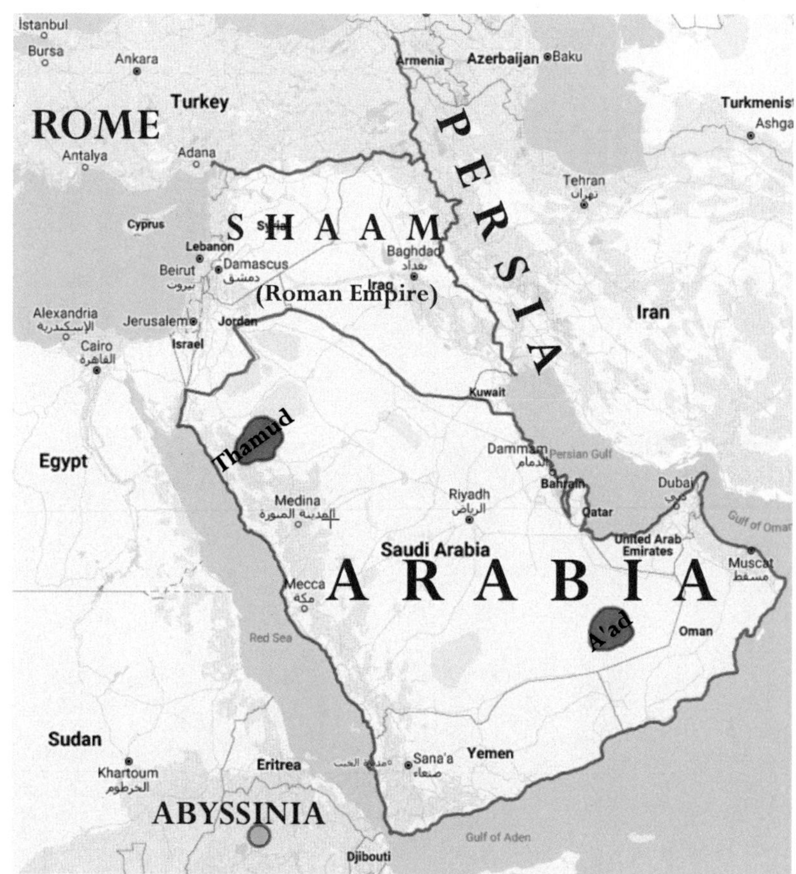

Pre-Islamic Traits of the Arabs

Negative Traits	Positive Traits
Gang-like Clans	Hospitality
Treatment of Women	Kept Promises
Marital Rights, Inheritance, Infanticide	Simple Lives
Gambling	Language
Heavy Drinking	Memory

Important Points
All people have good and bad qualities Proof of Islam found in how it transformed a society like this and took over the world

Pre-Islam: Quraysh Tribe and Control of Mecca

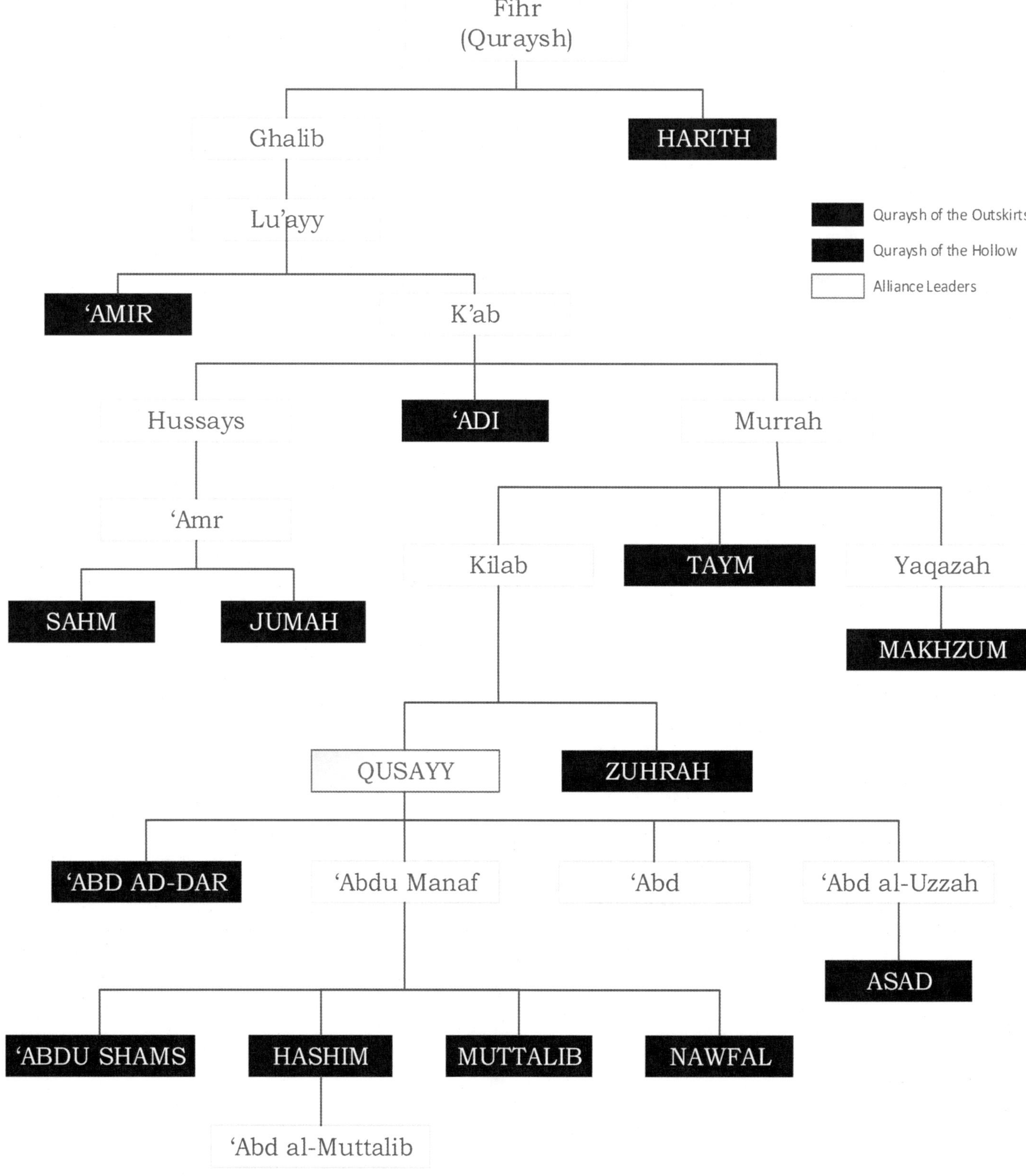

Pre-Islam: Quraysh Tribe and Control of Mecca

Qusayy from the tribe of Quraysh took control of Mecca

- Qusayy established certain responsibilities for the Quraysh as the people in control of Mecca
    - Siqāyah: supplying water to the pilgrims
    - Rifādah: providing food to the pilgrims
    - I'mārah: constructing and maintaining the haram
    - Sifārah: managing diplomatic affairs
    - Nadwah: conducting meetings and planning
    - Liwāa': holding the flag in war

'Abd Manaf

- His real name was Mugheerah

Hashim ibn 'Abd Manaf

Hashim ibn 'Abd Manaf

- Relation to the Prophet Muhammad ﷺ

- His Generosity

- His marriage and child

- His death in Gaza

Hashim ibn 'Abd Manaf

Under the leadership of Hashim, Mecca became a commercial business hub.

- He initiated the sending of two trade caravans a year to the north and south

بِسۡمِ اللّٰهِ الرَّحۡمٰنِ الرَّحِيۡمِ

لِاِيۡلٰفِ قُرَيۡشٍ ﴿۱﴾ اٖلٰفِهِمۡ رِحۡلَةَ الشِّتَآءِ وَ الصَّيۡفِ ﴿۲﴾ فَلۡيَعۡبُدُوۡا رَبَّ هٰذَا الۡبَيۡتِ ﴿۳﴾

الَّذِىۡۤ اَطۡعَمَهُمۡ مِّنۡ جُوۡعٍ ۙ وَّ اٰمَنَهُمۡ مِّنۡ خَوۡفٍ ﴿۴﴾

(With the grace of Allah) Due to the habituated custom of the Quraysh, their habitual custom of setting forth in winter and summer, (as a form of gratitude), they should worship Allah, the Lord of this house, He who has fed them against hunger and shielded them from fear. [106:1-4]

Abdul Muttalib

Abdul Muttalib

- Relation to Prophet Muhammad ﷺ

- Maintenance of many Abrahamic Traditions

- His rediscovery of the Well of ZamZam

- Abdul Muttalib's 10 sons

Abdul Muttalib

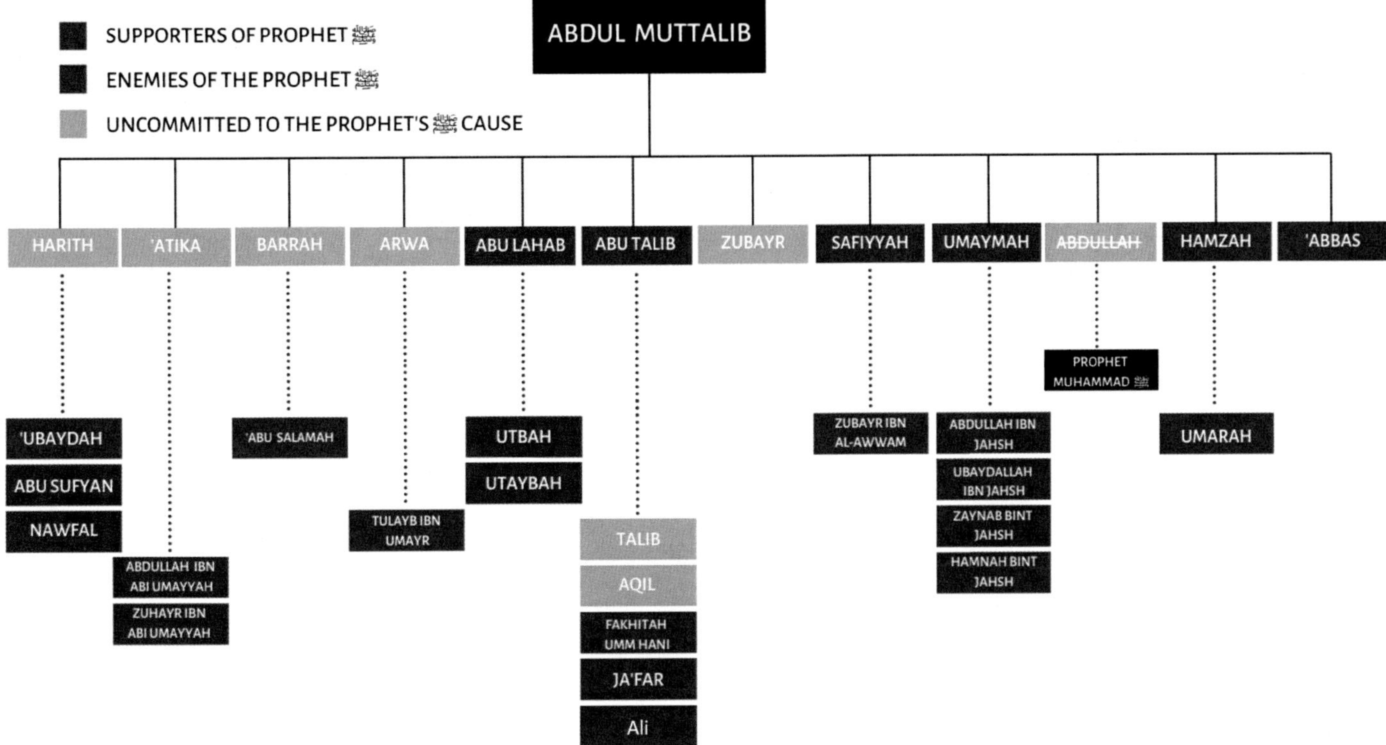
SUPPORTERS OF PROPHET ﷺ
ENEMIES OF THE PROPHET ﷺ
UNCOMMITTED TO THE PROPHET'S ﷺ CAUSE
ABDUL MUTTALIB
HARITH
'ATIKA
BARRAH
ARWA
ABU LAHAB
ABU TALIB
ZUBAYR
SAFIYYAH
UMAYMAH
ABDULLAH
HAMZAH
'ABBAS
'UBAYDAH
ABU SUFYAN
NAWFAL
ABDULLAH IBN ABI UMAYYAH
ZUHAYR IBN ABI UMAYYAH
'ABU SALAMAH
TULAYB IBN UMAYR
UTBAH
UTAYBAH
TALIB
AQIL
FAKHITAH UMM HANI
JA'FAR
Ali
ZUBAYR IBN AL-AWWAM
ABDULLAH IBN JAHSH
UBAYDALLAH IBN JAHSH
ZAYNAB BINT JAHSH
HAMNAH BINT JAHSH
PROPHET MUHAMMAD ﷺ
UMARAH

Prophet Muhammad's ﷺ Parents

The Prophet's ﷺ Father: Abdullah ibn Abdul Muttalib

- His marriage to Aaminah

The Prophet's ﷺ Mother: Aaminah bint Wahb

- Father is the chief of Banu Zahra

Umm Ayman

كَانَ النَّبِي صَلَّى اللَّهُ عَلَيْهِ وَسَلَّمَ يَقُوْلُ " أُمُّ أَيْمَن أُمِّي بَعْدَ أُمِّي" :

The Prophet ﷺ used to say "Umm Ayman is my mother after my mother."

Prophet Muhammad's W Lineage

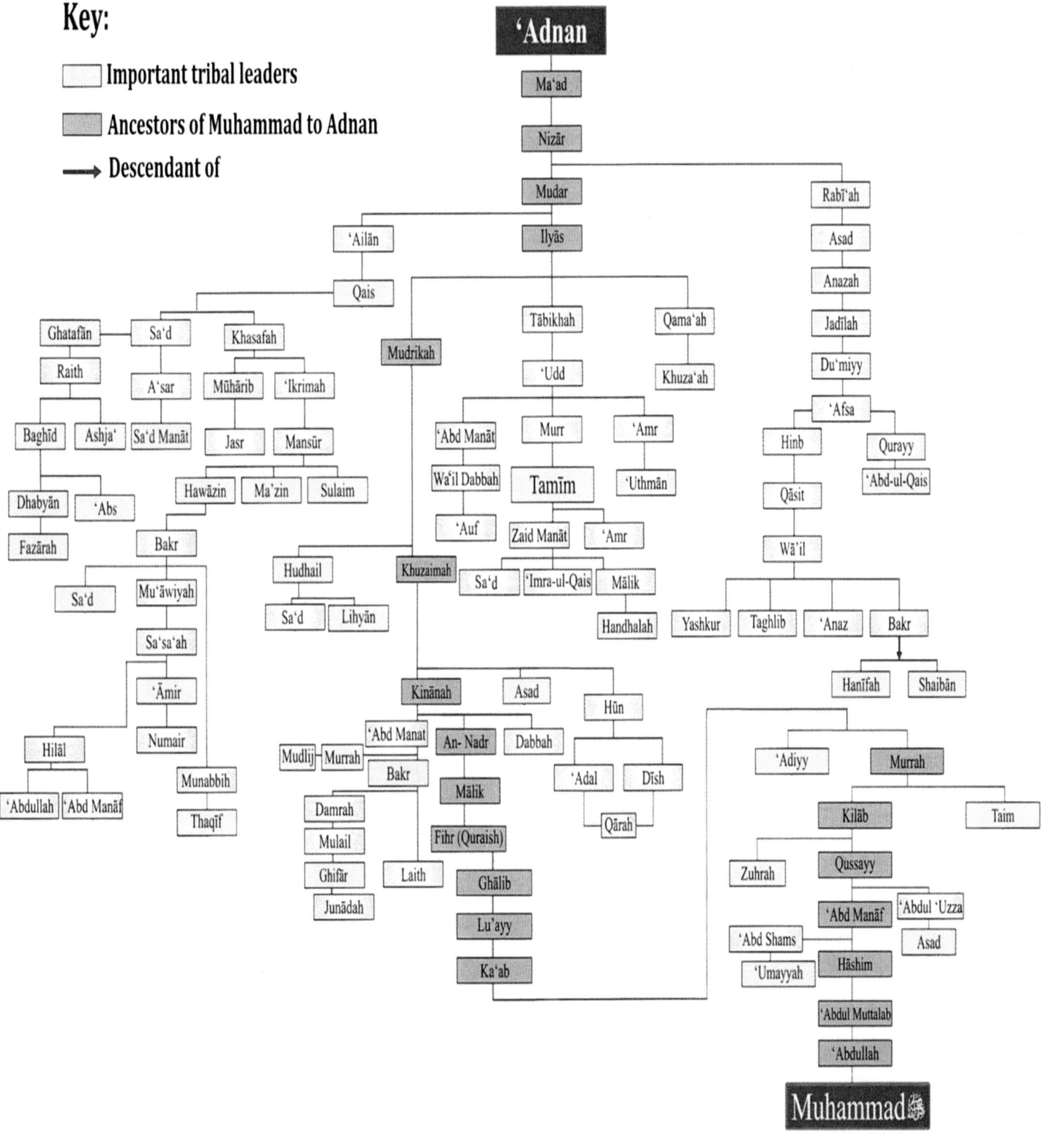

Phase Review Questions

1. How is the Prophet ﷺ connected to Ibrahim (AS) ?

2. What are a few similarities they had?

3. What was Hashim's real name and why was he given the name Hashim?

4. What was one reason Abdul Muttalib was so beloved to the Quraysh?

5. Who was the tenth son of Abdul Muttalib and why did he intend to slaughter him?

6. Who were the uncles of the Prophet ﷺ who supported Islam?

BIRTH AND EARLY LIFE

BIRTH AND EARLY LIFE

- Abraha and the Army of Elephants
- Miracles Before Prophet Muhammad's ﷺ Birth
- Prophet Muhammad's ﷺ Birth
- Naming and 'Aqiqah
- Names of the Prophet ﷺ
- Under the Care of Halima
- Splitting of the Prophet's ﷺ Chest
- Time with Aaminah bint Wahab
- Time with Abdul Muttalib
- Under Abu Talib's Care
- Phase Review Questions

Abraha and the Army of Elephants

Story of the Elephant

بِسۡمِ اللّٰهِ الرَّحۡمٰنِ الرَّحِیۡمِ

اَلَمۡ تَرَ كَیۡفَ فَعَلَ رَبُّكَ بِاَصۡحٰبِ الۡفِیۡلِ ﴿۱﴾ اَلَمۡ یَجۡعَلۡ كَیۡدَهُمۡ فِیۡ تَضۡلِیۡلٍ ﴿۲﴾
وَّ اَرۡسَلَ عَلَیۡهِمۡ طَیۡرًا اَبَابِیۡلَ ﴿۳﴾ تَرۡمِیۡهِمۡ بِحِجَارَةٍ مِّنۡ سِجِّیۡلٍ ﴿۴﴾ فَجَعَلَهُمۡ
كَعَصۡفٍ مَّاۡكُوۡلٍ ﴿۵﴾

Have you not seen how your Lord dealt with the People of the Elephant? (1) Has He not turned their plan into nullity? (2) And He sent upon them flying birds in flocks (3) throwing upon them stones of baked clay(4) and thus He turned them into an eaten-up chaff (5) [105:1-5]

Miracles before Prophet Muhammad's ﷺ Birth

Miracles

- Collapse of the 14 turrets of Kisra's Palace

- The Magician's Fire was extinguished

- Lake Sawah was dried up

(Al-Bayhaqī)

What was the purpose of these miracles?

Prophet Muhammad's ﷺ Birth

Born in the month of Rabi' Al-Awal in the Year of The Elephant

Miracles Experienced During His ﷺ Birth

- A dream in which a light was emitted from Aaminah that illuminated the palaces of Sham
- No pain during the pregnancy

The Quraysh were overcome with joy at his birth ﷺ

- Abu Lahab freed his slave Thuwaybah after she gave him the news of the Prophet's ﷺ birth
- Abdul Muttalib was ecstatic
- Quraysh knew he ﷺ was special from an early age

Naming and 'Aqiqah

Abdul Muttalib performed the Aqiqah on the 7th day after birth and invited all of Quraysh.

Aaminah and Abdul Muttalib were inspired with dreams to name him Muhammad ﷺ.

Muhammad: from the root letters of حمد

- Refers to a person of praiseworthy attributes whose practical virtues, indisputable achievements, and outstanding character, are repeatedly glorified.

اَللّٰهُمَّ صَلِّ عَلَى مُحَمَّدٍ وَّعَلَى صَحْبِهٖ وَ بَارِكْ وَسَلِّمْ

O Allah! Shower Your blessings upon Muhammad and his family and companions accompanied by blessings and peace.

- Known in previous books as Ahmad

وَ اِذْ قَالَ عِيْسَى ابْنُ مَرْيَمَ يٰبَنِيْٓ اِسْرَآءِيْلَ اِنِّيْ رَسُوْلُ اللّٰهِ اِلَيْكُمْ مُّصَدِّقًا لِّمَا بَيْنَ يَدَيَّ
مِنَ التَّوْرٰىةِ وَ مُبَشِّرًاۢ بِرَسُوْلٍ يَّاْتِيْ مِنْۢ بَعْدِى اسْمُهٗٓ اَحْمَدُ ؕ

And when 'Isa Ibn Maryam said: "O People of Israa'eel! I am a messenger of Allah unto you, confirming the Torah (that appeared) before me and (a messenger) of glad tidings of a prophet to come after me, whose name shall be Ahmad." [61:6]

Names of the Prophet ﷺ

The Prophet ﷺ had many names

The Prophet Muhammad ﷺsaid :

سَمُّوا بِاسْمِى

Name your children with my name. [Bukhari]

Sunnan after a baby is born include:

Under the Care of Halima

The children of the Arabs would often be sent to the desert in their nursery years.

- This would have profound effects on their character
- The city had a mix of people and languages
- The desert held the purest of the Arabs
- The desert would allow the child to become tough
- The language was pure and eloquent
- They learned life skills early on

Halima Al-Sa'diyah and her tribe came to Mecca to receive the new batch of children.

Miracles experienced by Halima and her husband Harith, or Abu Kabshah

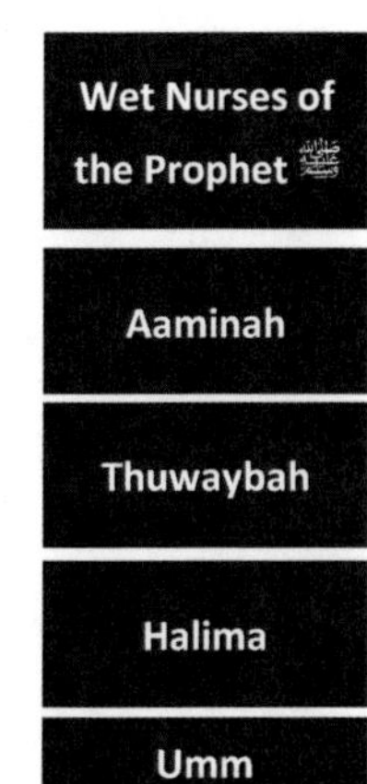

Wet Nurses of the Prophet ﷺ
Aaminah
Thuwaybah
Halima
Umm Hamzah

Splitting of the Prophet's ﷺ Chest

The first time Prophet Muhammad's ﷺ chest was split was in the care of Halima

- Two dark spots were removed from the Prophet's ﷺ heart
- The Prophet's ﷺ inner body was cleansed with snow and cold water

After the incident, Halima returned him to Aaminah and informed her of what happened

- Halima was worried that something bad happened to the Prophet ﷺ, but Aaminah knew that the Prophet ﷺ was protected.

Splitting of the Prophet's ﷺ Chest

The Prophet 's ﷺ heart was split a total of 4 times

- First: Under the care of Halima (4 or 5 years old)
- Second: 10 years old
- Third: First Revelation (40 years old)
- Fourth: Before the night journey (51 years old)

Time with Aaminah bint Wahab

After returning home. Muhammad ﷺ was under the care of his mother Aaminah until the age of 6

Aaminah traveled with Muhammad ﷺ to Yathrib along with Umm Ayman.

On their return back to Mecca, Aaminah passed away in a place called Abwa.

What is the final fate of the parents of the Prophet ﷺ?

6 yrs. After Birth

Abdullah	Aaminah	Abdul Muttalib	Qasim	Khadija & Abu Talib	Ruqayyah	Hamzah	Zainab & Umm Kulthoom	Ibrahim

Time with Abdul Muttalib

8

Umm Ayman returned to Mecca with the Prophet ﷺ.

The Guardianship of Abdul Muttalib

The Death of Abdul Muttalib

8 yrs. After Birth

Abdullah	Aaminah	Abdul Muttalib	Qasim	Khadija & Abu Talib	Ruqayyah	Hamzah	Zainab & Umm Kulthoom	Ibrahim

Under Abu Talib's Care

The Prophet ﷺ was very beloved to Abu Talib. Abu Talib preferred him over his own children.

Abu Talib would often recite the following couplet:

وَشُقَّ لَهُ مِنْ اِسْمِهِ لِيُجِلَّهُ فَذُو الْعَرْشِ مَحمُوْدٌ وَهٰذَا مُحَمَّدٌ

Allah has extracted his (Muhammad's) name from His own so that he may be exalted,

So the one on the throne is Mahmood whilst this is Muhammad.

The Prayer for Rain

The Journey to Syria and Bahira the Monk

Bahira witnessed many miracles and recognized that Muhammad ﷺ was a prophet of Allah

- A cloud providing shade to the caravan
- Rocks and trees performing sujood
- Shade of a tree leaning towards him
- Seal of Prophethood

Phase Review Questions

1. How old was the Prophet ﷺ when his father passed away? His mother?

2. What was the most prominent event before the birth of the Prophet ﷺ ?

3. What was one miracle which took place before/during his birth ﷺ ?

4. What does Muhammad mean? Was this a common name?

5. Why would the Arabs send their kids to the desert for nursing?

6. What is one miracle Halima experienced when caring for the Prophet ﷺ ?

Phase Review Questions

7. How many times was the Prophet's ﷺ heart opened?

8. When and where did Aaminah pass away?

9. How old was the Prophet ﷺ when Abdul Muttalib passed away?

10. Who was the monk that recognized the Prophet ﷺ? What is one miracle he saw?

11. What is a trait that all of the prophets (AS) shared and what was the wisdom behind it?

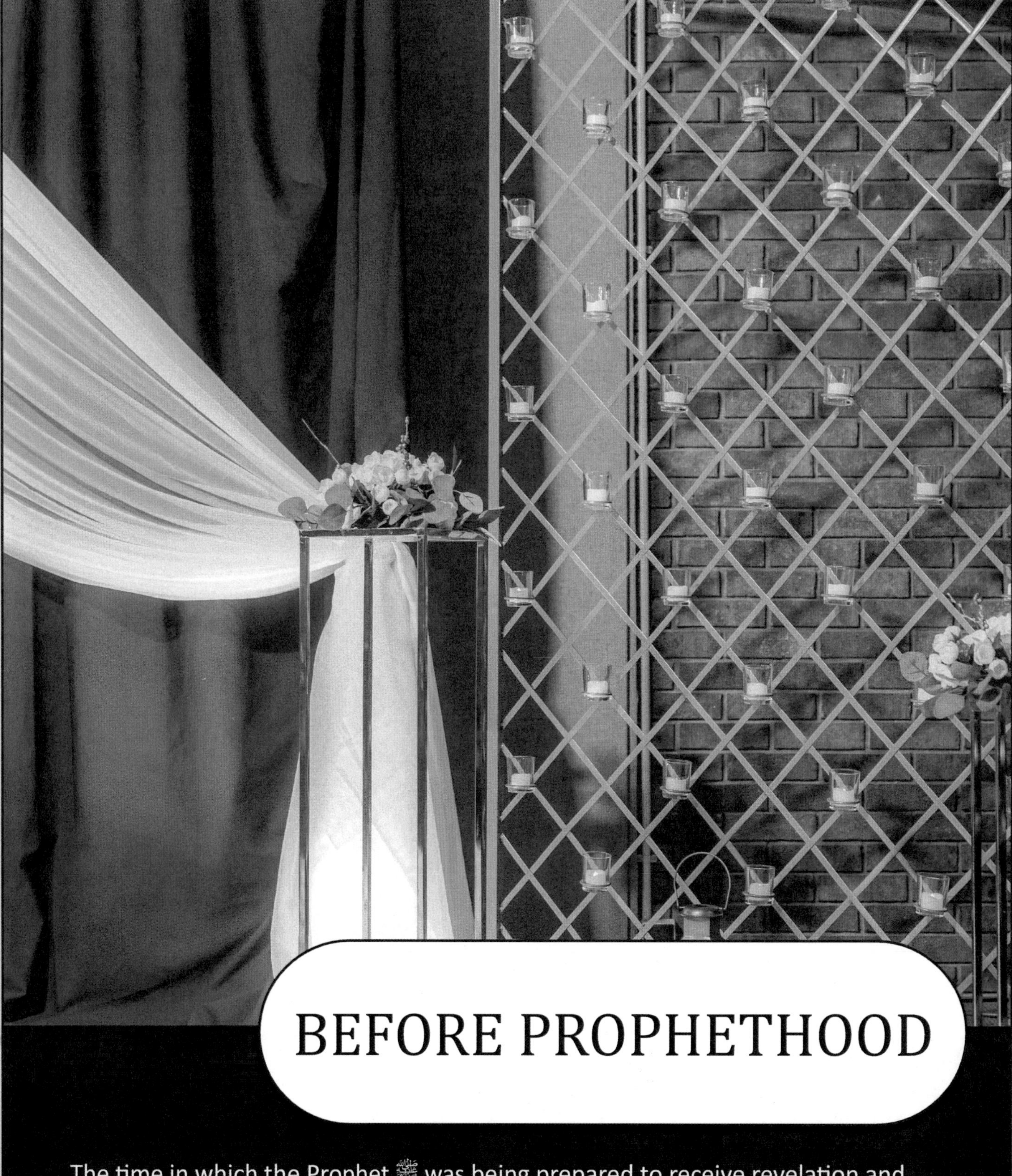

BEFORE PROPHETHOOD

The time in which the Prophet ﷺ was being prepared to receive revelation and was establishing himself in the Meccan society.

BEFORE PROPHETHOOD

- Early Teenage Years
- Harb Al-Fijar
- Hilf ul-Fudhul
- Time as a Merchant
- The Marriage Proposal
- Marriage to Khadijah bint Khuwaylid RA
- The Virtues of Khadijah bint Khuwaylid RA
- Household of the Prophet ﷺ
- Rebuilding the Ka'bah
- Hunafa Before Islam
- Phase Review Questions

Early Teenage Years

Divine Protection from Allah SWT

- The Prophet ﷺ never worshiped idols or consumed alcohol

- The Prophet ﷺ would not eat anything slaughtered in the name of an idol

Prophet Muhammad ﷺ as a Shepherd

- This is a role which all of the Prophets (AS) shared

عَنْ أَبِي هُرَيْرَةَ عَنْ النَّبِيِّ W قَالَ مَا بَعَثَ اللَّهُ نَبِيًّا إِلَّا رَعَى الْغَنَمَ

It was narrated by Abu Hurayrah that the Prophet W *said, "Allah did not send any prophet except that he took care of sheep." [Bukhari]*

Traits and Benefits of Being a Shepherd

Harb Al-Fijar

When the Prophet ﷺ was 20 years old, a war erupted between Quraysh and the tribe of Qays.

- A man from Kinanah, named Al-Barrad, killed a man from Qays, named 'Urwa ibn Qays
- Quraysh allied with Kinanah and fought against Qays

This was an extremely violent war that lasted 4 years.

- The fighting continued even in the forbidden months of the year. This is why it was named Harb Al-Fijar
- Forbidden Months:
- Fijar means:
- At the end of this war people realized there was a need to stop these violent wars.

Hilf ul-Fudhul

Took place in the month of Dhul Qa'da

- A defenseless man from Yemen was treated wrongly in a business transaction. A Qurayshi took his goods and there were no repercussions.

- A meeting was held in the house of Abdullah ibn Jud'an with many honorable leaders of Quraysh.

The pact stated:

- We will stand with the oppressed person, regardless of who they are, until their right is returned to them.

Hilf Ul-Fudhul means:

The Prophet W was also present and praised the occasion after Prophethood.

"If I were called to this pact in Islam I would accept it".

Time as a Merchant

25

When Prophet Muhammad ﷺ entered into transactions, he was the most truthful and honest . He became known as Al-Amin.

- He was known to have never told a lie and people would entrust him with their valuable things even after they became his enemies.

At 25, Khadijah (RA) requested him to take her goods to Shaam (Syria) for trade.

- She was informed about him initially through her sister Hala.

Maysarah and Nestor the Monk

The Marriage Proposal

Khadijah (RA) developed a longing to marry the Prophet ﷺ, so she sent him a proposal.

- Khadijah (RA) sent Nafisah bint Munayya to propose on her behalf

Khadijah (RA) was 40 and the Prophet ﷺ was 25 when they got married.

- Khadijah (RA) had been widowed twice
- Khadijah (RA) previously had three children
- Abu Talib was the representative of the Prophet ﷺ and Khadijah's uncle was her representative
- Her dowry was 20 camels

Marriage to Khadijah bint Khuwaylid (RA)

25

The Relationship between Khadijah (RA) and the Prophet ﷺ

- Khadijah's (RA) words to him when the Prophet ﷺ accepted her marriage proposal

- Khadijah (RA) was the first wife of Prophet ﷺ and he ﷺ did not marry another woman until she passed away 25 years later.

- The Prophet ﷺ loved her very much, especially because she (RA) believed in his Prophethood without hesitation.

The Virtues of Khadijah bint Khuwaylid (RA)

Jibreel conveyed Allah's SWT Salam to Khadijah.

Khadijah's necklace

Aisha (RA) and Khadijah (RA)

- The Prophet ﷺ said: *"Allah SWT did not give me a wife better than Khadijah"*.

- The Prophet ﷺ would make effort to take care of Khadijah's (RA) family and friends after she passed away.
- He ﷺ would slaughter animals and give the meat to those close to Khadijah (RA)

Household of the Prophet ﷺ

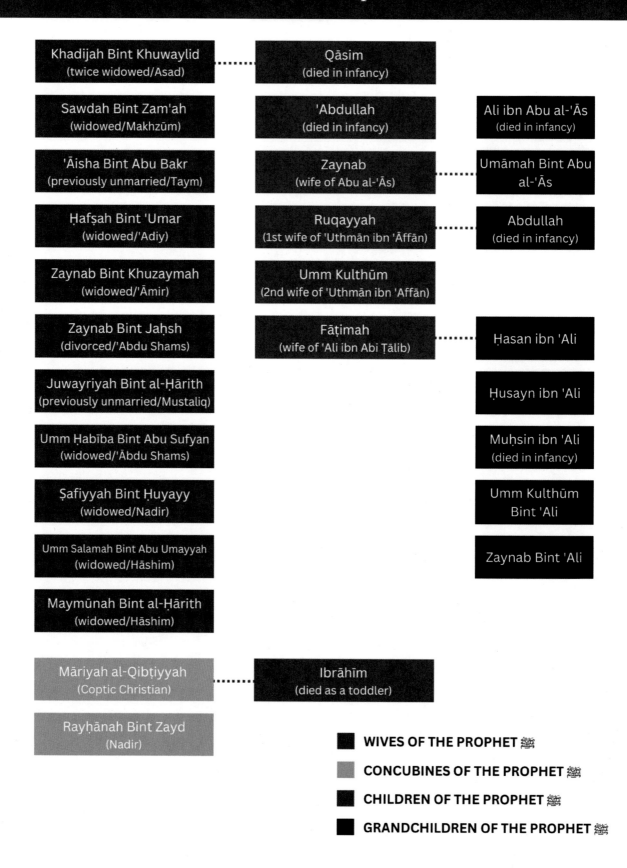

Wives / Concubines	Children	Grandchildren
Khadijah Bint Khuwaylid (twice widowed/Asad)	Qāsim (died in infancy)	
Sawdah Bint Zam'ah (widowed/Makhzūm)	'Abdullah (died in infancy)	Ali ibn Abu al-'Ās (died in infancy)
'Āisha Bint Abu Bakr (previously unmarried/Taym)	Zaynab (wife of Abu al-'Ās)	Umāmah Bint Abu al-'Ās
Ḥafṣah Bint 'Umar (widowed/'Adiy)	Ruqayyah (1st wife of 'Uthmān ibn 'Āffān)	Abdullah (died in infancy)
Zaynab Bint Khuzaymah (widowed/'Āmir)	Umm Kulthūm (2nd wife of 'Uthmān ibn 'Affān)	
Zaynab Bint Jaḥsh (divorced/'Abdu Shams)	Fāṭimah (wife of 'Ali ibn Abi Ṭālib)	Ḥasan ibn 'Ali
Juwayriyah Bint al-Ḥārith (previously unmarried/Mustaliq)		Ḥusayn ibn 'Ali
Umm Ḥabība Bint Abu Sufyan (widowed/'Ābdu Shams)		Muḥsin ibn 'Ali (died in infancy)
Ṣafiyyah Bint Ḥuyayy (widowed/Nadir)		Umm Kulthūm Bint 'Ali
Umm Salamah Bint Abu Umayyah (widowed/Hāshim)		Zaynab Bint 'Ali
Maymūnah Bint al-Ḥārith (widowed/Hāshim)		
Māriyah al-Qibṭiyyah (Coptic Christian)	Ibrāhīm (died as a toddler)	
Rayḥānah Bint Zayd (Nadir)		

- WIVES OF THE PROPHET ﷺ
- CONCUBINES OF THE PROPHET ﷺ
- CHILDREN OF THE PROPHET ﷺ
- GRANDCHILDREN OF THE PROPHET ﷺ

Household of the Prophet ﷺ

Khadijah (RA) was the only wife to have children with Prophet Muhammad ﷺ. They had 6 children:

- Al Qasim:

- Zaynab (RA):

- Ruqayyah (RA):

- Umm Kulthum (RA):

- Fatima (RA):

- ‘Abdullah (Tayyib/Tahir):

Household of the Prophet ﷺ

Additional Members:

- Zaid ibn Haritha (RA):

- Ali ibn Abi Talib (RA):

Rebuilding the Ka'bah

إِنَّ أَوَّلَ بَيْتٍ وُضِعَ لِلنَّاسِ لَلَّذِي بِبَكَّةَ مُبَارَكًا وَهُدًى لِّلْعَالَمِينَ ﴿٩٦﴾

The first house built for the people is the one in Bakkah, blessed and a guidance for the worlds [3:96]

When the Prophet ﷺ was 35 years old, the Quraysh wanted to rebuild the Ka'bah.

- It was originally roofless and low in height
- There was easy access to the valuables inside of it
- It began to crack and fall apart

When the building was almost complete, an intense dispute broke out regarding which party would have the honor of placing the Black Stone.

هٰذَا مُحَمَّدٌ الْأَمِيْنُ رَضِيْنَا هٰذَا مُحَمَّدٌ الْأَمِيْنُ

This is Muhammad, the trustworthy. We are extremely pleased with him as arbiter.
This is after all Muhammad, the trustworthy.

Hunafa Before Islam

There were many people still upon the religion of Ibrahim (AS) and upon pure monotheism in Mecca.

- Zaid ibn 'Amr

- Abu Bakr (RA)

- Uthman (RA)

Hunafa from Banu Asad

- Khadijah (RA)

- Waraqa ibn Nawfal

Phase Review Questions

1. What evils did Allah SWT protect the Prophet ﷺ from before he received revelation?

2. Describe the war that took place when the Prophet ﷺ was 20 years old.

3. What were the ethics detailed in the Hilf ul-Fudhul pact?

4. What was the Prophet ﷺ known as in Mecca? How did he earn this name?

5. How did Khadijah (RA) first hear about the Prophet ﷺ ?

6. Who was the servant who accompanied Prophet Muhammad ﷺ on Khadijah's (RA) business trip?

7. How old were Khadijah (RA) and the Prophet ﷺ when they were married? Who proposed the

Phase Review Questions

8. Who gave the speech at the marriage?

9. List the names of the Prophet's ﷺ children:

10. How many of his ﷺ children passed away before him?

11. Why was the Ka'bah rebuilt?

12. What were the tribes disputing about?

13. What does it mean to be a "Haneef"?

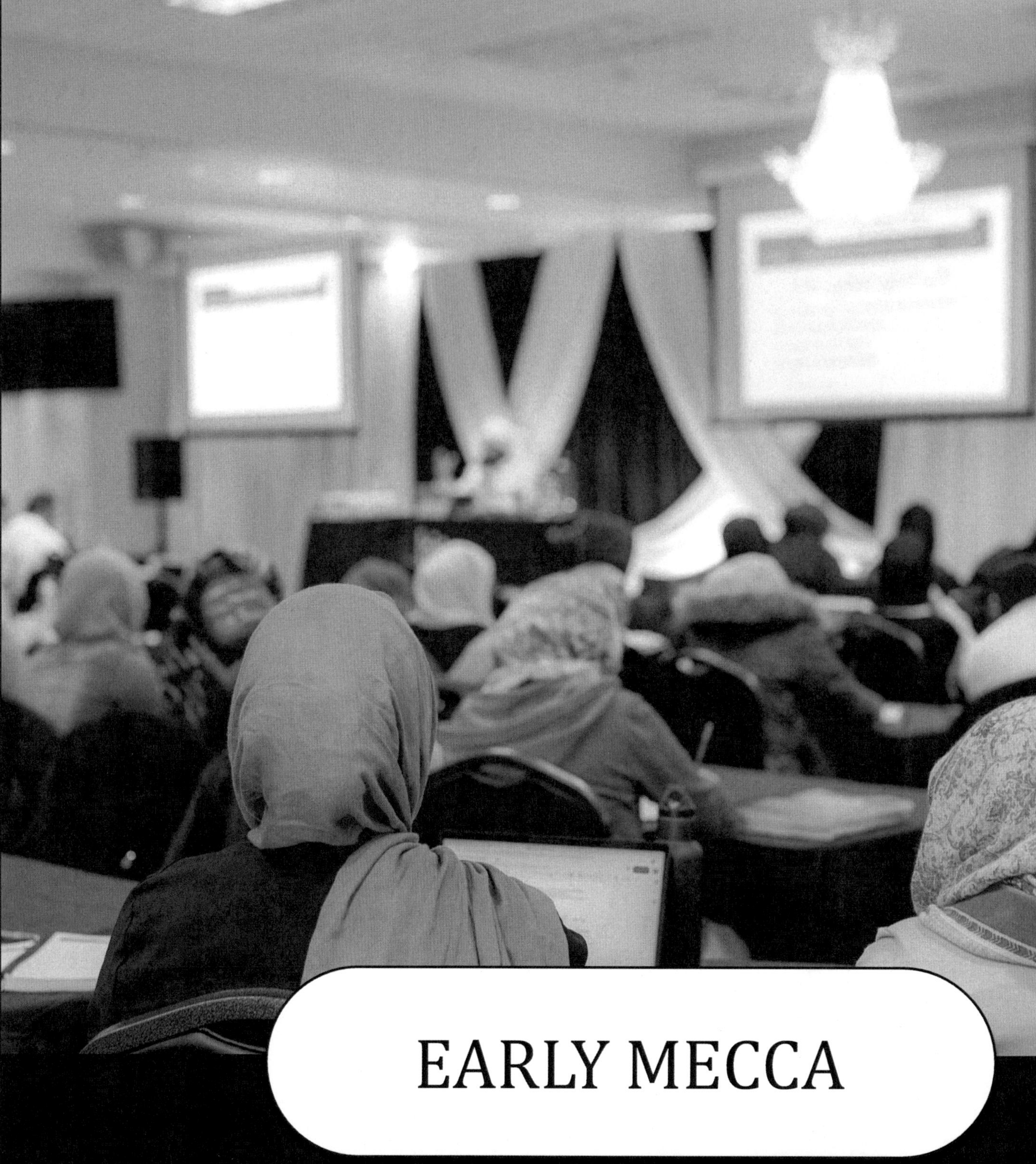

EARLY MECCA

A time of secrecy, with a gradual increase in the followers of Islam, and extreme hardship for the Muslims.

EARLY MECCA

- Prophethood Map
- Pre-Revelation Events
- First Revelation
- Khadijah's (RA) Response
- Modes of Revelation
- The Prophet's ﷺ Relationship with Jibreel
- Next Revelations
- First Converts
- The Quiet Call to Islam
- Early Converts
- Dar Al-Arqam
- Open Call to Islam
- Response from the People of Quraysh
- Effect of the Quran on Non-Muslims
- Negotiations of Quraysh
- Assessment from Quraysh and the Jews
- Hostility of Quraysh
- Persecution of Muslims

EARLY MECCA

- Enemies of the Prophet ﷺ
- Quraysh's Tactics Against the Prophet ﷺ
- Migration to Abyssinia
- Hamza's (RA) Conversion
- 'Umar ibn al-Khattab's (RA) Conversion
- Phase Review Questions

Prophethood Map

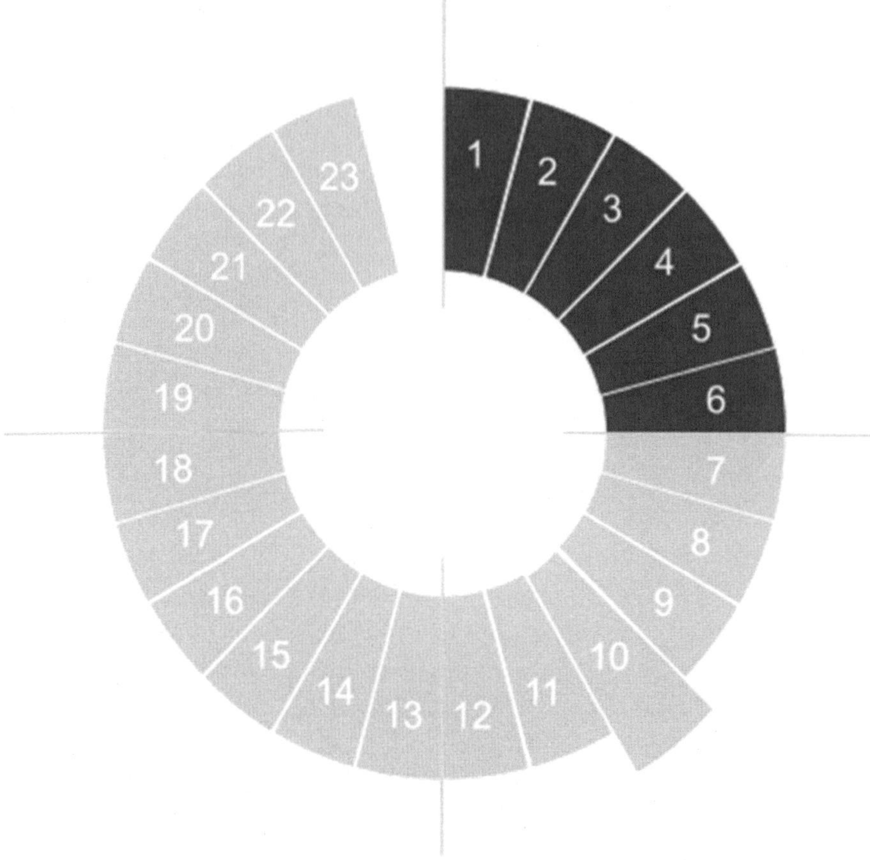

Private Assembly

The first three years of the Prophet's ﷺ message are limited to private gatherings.

Public Invitation

The Prophet ﷺ opens up his message to his extended family and the rest of the Quraysh.

Abyssinia

Several early converts migrate to Abyssinia seeking political Asylum.

Conversions of Hamzah (RA) and 'Umar (RA)

Hamzah (RA) and 'Umar (RA) become two pivotal supporters who come to the Prophet's ﷺ aid.

Pre-Revelation Events

Before Revelation, the Prophet ﷺ was protected from any type of polytheism.

As the time for revelation drew closer, the Prophet ﷺ began to have truthful and pious dreams.

- Pious dreams = 1/26th of Prophethood

Stones, trees, and mountains would greet him ﷺ and he ﷺ would hear voices and see light.

He would go to the Cave of Hira for seclusion – for dhikr, meditation, and reflection.

'Aisha (RA) said:

اَوَّلَ مَا بَدَئ بِهِ رَسُوْلُ اللهِ صَلَى اللهُ عَلَيْهِ وَسَلَّمْ مِنَ الْوَحِىْ الرُّؤْيَا الصَّالِحَةُ فِي النُّوْمِ فَكَانَ لَا يَرَى
رُؤْيَا الْاَجَاءَتْ مِثْلَ فَلَقَ الصُّبْح

Divine revelation upon the Messenger of Allah ﷺ originated with pious dreams. Whatever he witnessed in his dreams, it would come to pass as true as the crack of dawn. [Bukhari]

Pre-Revelation Events

Ummul-Muminīn, 'Aisha (RA) further relates:

ثُمَّ حَبَّبَ اِلَيْهِ الْخَلَا وَ كَانَ يَخْلُوْ بِغَارِ حِرَاء

Thereafter, solitude was made dear to him. He would often go into seclusion in the cave of Hira.

Imam Al-Bukhari narrates a Hadith in which 'Aisha (RA) mentions how the Prophet (RA) would act in the early stages of revelation.

"At first he would see true dreams at night, they would be as clear as the daybreak. Then he began to enjoy seclusion, he would go to Hira and worship in it for many days before returning to Mecca…"

First Revelation

Date of First Revelation

- Hafiz ibn 'Abd al-Barr: 8th Rabi' al-Awwal
- Ibn Ishaq & Ibn Hajar: 17th Ramadan

Story of First Revelation

- The Cave of Hira

- Jibreel came in the cave and said: اِقْرَأْ

First Revelation

- Prophet ﷺ replied:

مَا أنَا بِقَارِئ

I am unable to read

- First 5 verses of Surah Alaq were revealed:

اِقْرَأ بِاسْمِ رَبِّكَ الَّذِىْ خَلَقَ ﴿١﴾ خَلَقَ الْاِنْسَانَ مِنْ عَلَقٍ ﴿٢﴾ اِقْرَأ وَ رَبُّكَ الْاَكْرَمُ ﴿٣﴾
الَّذِىْ عَلَّمَ بِالْقَلَمِ ﴿٤﴾ عَلَّمَ الْاِنْسَانَ مَا لَمْ يَعْلَمْ ﴿٥﴾

Read (with the aid) of the name of your Lord Who has created (the entire universe). He has created (above all) man from a clot of blood. Read! And your Lord is the most gracious Who has taught (knowledge) by the use of the pen. He has taught man that which he did not know. [96:1-5]

Khadijah's (RA) Response

After the incident at the Cave of Hira, Prophet Muhammad ﷺ returns to Khadijah (RA)

فَدَخَلَ عَلَى خَدِيجَةَ بِنْتِ خُوَيْلِدٍ رَضِيَ اللهُ عَنْهَا فَقَالَ " زَمِّلُونِي زَمِّلُونِي ". فَزَمَّلُوهُ حَتَّى ذَهَبَ عَنْهُ الرَّوْعُ، فَقَالَ لِخَدِيجَةَ وَأَخْبَرَهَا الْخَبَرَ " لَقَدْ خَشِيتُ عَلَى نَفْسِي " فَقَالَتْ خَدِيجَةُ كَلاَّ وَاللهِ مَا يُخْزِيكَ اللهُ أَبَدًا، إِنَّكَ لَتَصِلُ الرَّحِمَ، وَتَحْمِلُ الْكَلَّ، وَتَكْسِبُ الْمَعْدُومَ، وَتَقْرِي الضَّيْفَ، وَتُعِينُ عَلَى نَوَائِبِ الْحَقِّ

Then he went to Khadijah bint Khuwailid (RA) and said, "Cover me! Cover me!" They covered him till his fear was over, and after that he told her everything that had happened and said, "I fear that something may happen to me." Khadijah replied, "Never! By Allah, Allah will never disgrace you. You keep good relations with your kith and kin, help the poor and the destitute, serve your guests generously, and assist the deserving calamity-afflicted ones." [Bukhari]

Khadijah (RA) takes the Prophet ﷺ to consult with her cousin Waraqa.

Modes of Revelation

Revelation came in the life of the Prophet ﷺ in various modes:

- True Dreams/Visions

- Revelation being placed into the heart of the Prophet ﷺ without physical interaction

- From angels appearing in a human form

- Sounds like the ringing of a bell

- Seeing angels in their true form

- Revelation without mediation

- Witnessing Allah SWT directly

The Prophet's ﷺ Relationship with Jibreel

- The Prophet ﷺ described Jibreel in hadith

- He ﷺ had a very close relationship with Jibreel

- He ﷺ would seek the advice of Jibreel

Next Revelations

After revelation, there was a period of time in which revelation stopped.

- Difference of Opinion

Next Revelations

- Muzzammil

- Muddathir

- Qalam

بِسۡمِ اللّٰهِ الرَّحۡمٰنِ الرَّحِيۡمِ
يٰۤاَيُّهَا الۡمُزَّمِّلُ ﴿۱﴾ قُمِ الَّيۡلَ اِلَّا قَلِيۡلًا ﴿۲﴾ نِّصۡفَهٗۤ اَوِ انۡقُصۡ مِنۡهُ قَلِيۡلًا ﴿۳﴾
اَوۡ زِدۡ عَلَيۡهِ وَ رَتِّلِ الۡقُرۡاٰنَ تَرۡتِيۡلًا ﴿۴﴾ اِنَّا سَنُلۡقِىۡ عَلَيۡكَ قَوۡلًا ثَقِيۡلًا ﴿۵﴾

O you, wrapped up in clothes (1) stand at night (for prayer) except a little (2) half of it, or make it a little less (3) or make it a little more and recite the Quran clearly with tarteel (in a distinct and measured tone) (4) We are going to send down to you a weighty discourse (5) [73:1-5]

Next Revelations

بِسۡمِ اللّٰهِ الرَّحۡمٰنِ الرَّحِيۡمِ
يٰۤاَيُّهَا الۡمُدَّثِّرُ ﴿١﴾ قُمۡ فَاَنۡذِرۡ ﴿٢﴾ وَ رَبَّكَ فَكَبِّرۡ ﴿٣﴾ وَ ثِيَابَكَ فَطَهِّرۡ ﴿٤﴾ وَ
الرُّجۡزَ فَاهۡجُرۡ ﴿٥﴾ وَ لَا تَمۡنُنۡ تَسۡتَكۡثِرُ ﴿٦﴾
وَ لِرَبِّكَ فَاصۡبِرۡ ﴿٧﴾ فَاِذَا نُقِرَ فِي النَّاقُوۡرِ ﴿٨﴾ فَذٰلِكَ يَوۡمَئِذٍ يَّوۡمٌ عَسِيۡرٌ ﴿٩﴾
عَلَى الۡكٰفِرِيۡنَ غَيۡرُ يَسِيۡرٍ ﴿١٠﴾
ذَرۡنِيۡ وَ مَنۡ خَلَقۡتُ وَحِيۡدًا ﴿١١﴾

O you, enveloped in a mantle (1) stand up and warn (2) and pronounce the greatness of your Lord (3) and purify your clothes (4) and keep away from filth (5) and do not do a favor (to anyone merely) to seek more (in return) (6) And for the sake of your Lord, observe patience (7) For when the trumpet will be blown (8) that day will be a difficult day (9) not easy for the disbelievers (10) Leave me alone (to deal) with the one whom I created lonely (11) [74:1-11]

First Converts

First Converts of Islam

Khadijah (RA)

Abu Bakr as-Siddiq (RA)

- The first person outside of the household of the Prophet ﷺ to accept Islam

- He would purchase slaves and free them

- He placed himself in danger to protect the Prophet ﷺ

First Converts

Waraqa ibn Nawfal

Zaid ibn Harithah (RA)

The Family of Abu Talib

Imam Abu Hanifa (RH):

Amongst the free men it was Abu Bakr (RA). Amongst the women it was Khadijah (RA). The first slave to embrace Islam was Zaid ibn Haritha (RA) whilst Ali (RA) was the first child to come into the fold of Islam.

The Quiet Call to Islam

First Three Years of Prophethood

- The call to Islam was done privately during this time
- News leaked to Quraysh, but they paid little heed

Wudu and Prayer Taught to the Prophet ﷺ

Early Converts

- Many of the early converts were slaves, children, and poor people

Abu Bakr's (RA) Converts

- Uthman ibn 'Affan (RA)

- Az-Zubayr ibn 'Awwam (RA)

- 'Abdul Rahman ibn 'Awf (RA)

Early Converts

Abu Bakr's Converts

- Sa'd ibn Abi Waqqas (RA)

- Talha ibn 'Ubaydallah (RA)

- Sa'eed ibn Zayd (RA)

- Khalid ibn Sa'eed (RA)

Early Converts

Other Notable Converts

- Abdullah ibn Mas'ud (RA)

- Ja'far ibn Abi Talib (RA)

- Family of Yasir (RA)

- Suhaib ar-Rumi (RA)

- Arqam ibn Abi Arqam (RA)

Early Converts

Early converts from outside of Hijaz

- Abu Dharr (RA) - Ghifar

- Abu Musa Al-Ash'ari (RA) - Yemen

- Tufail ibn 'Amr (RA) - Daws (Tribe of Abu Huraira)
    - 10th Year of Prophethood

- 'Amr ibn 'Abasa (RA)

- Dhimad (RA)

Dar Al-Arqam

As the small group of Muslims increased, they decided to gather in the house of Arqam (RA)

Arqam (RA) and his Contribution

Lessons and Important Points

Open Call to Islam

Over a period of three years, Prophet Muhammad ﷺ continued to invite people to Islam as a steady stream of people embraced it.

After these three years, Prophet Muhammad ﷺ was instructed to proclaim this invitation openly. At this time, the following verses were revealed:

وَ اَنْذِرْ عَشِيْرَتَكَ الْاَقْرَبِيْنَ ﴿٢١۴﴾ وَ اخْفِضْ جَنَاحَكَ لِمَنِ اتَّبَعَكَ مِنَ الْمُؤْمِنِيْنَ ﴿٢١۵﴾

And warn your close relatives and treat with affection those believers who have followed you. [26:214-215]

فَاصْدَعْ بِمَا تُؤْمَرُ وَ اَعْرِضْ عَنِ الْمُشْرِكِيْنَ ﴿٩۴﴾

Therefore proclaim (Islam) openly that which you have been instructed and turn away from the disbelievers. [15:94]

وَ قُلْ اِنِّيْٓ اَنَا النَّذِيْرُ الْمُبِيْنُ ﴿٨٩﴾

And say (O Muhammad!) I am indeed an open warner. [15:89]

The Prophet ﷺ invited his kinsmen for a meal and called them to Islam.

Response from the People of Quraysh

The Prophet ﷺ warned his tribe atop Mt. Safa, whereupon Abu Lahab insulted him.

بِسْمِ اللهِ الرَّحْمٰنِ الرَّحِيْمِ
تَبَّتْ يَدَآ اَبِيْ لَهَبٍ وَّ تَبَّ ﴿١﴾ مَآ اَغْنٰى عَنْهُ مَالُهٗ وَ مَا كَسَبَ ﴿٢﴾
سَيَصْلٰى نَارًا ذَاتَ لَهَبٍ ﴿٣﴾
وَّ امْرَاَتُهٗ ؕ حَمَّالَةَ الْحَطَبِ ﴿٤﴾ فِيْ جِيْدِهَا حَبْلٌ مِّنْ مَّسَدٍ ﴿٥﴾

Perish the two hands of Abu Lahab, and perish he! (1) Neither his wealth benefited him, nor what he earned(2) He will soon enter a Fire, full of flames (3) and his wife as well, the wicked carrier of firewood (4) around her neck, there is (a collar of iron, like) a well twisted rope. (5) [111:1-5]

Effect of the Quran on Non-Muslims

The eloquence of the Quran was mesmerizing to even the most staunch enemies of Islam.

- Abu Jahl, Abu Sufyan, and Akhnas ibn Shurayq

- Utbah Ibn Abi Rabi'

- 'Uqbah Ibn Abi Mu'eet and Ummayah ibn Khalaf

    - Allah SWT revealed:

وَ يَوْمَ يَعَضُّ الظَّالِمُ عَلٰى يَدَيْهِ يَقُوْلُ يٰلَيْتَنِى اتَّخَذْتُ مَعَ الرَّسُوْلِ سَبِيْلًا ﴿٢٧﴾
يٰوَيْلَتٰى لَيْتَنِىْ لَمْ اَتَّخِذْ فُلَانًا خَلِيْلًا ﴿٢٨﴾

And (Be mindful of) the Day the wrongdoer will bite his hands saying, Would that I had taken a path along with the messenger! (27) Woe to me! Would that I had not taken so and so for my friend! (28) [25:27-28]

- Al-Waleed ibn Al-Mugheerah

Negotiations of the Quraysh with Abu Talib

The Quraysh began their attempts to stop Islam by making offers to Abu Talib

Abu Talib affirmed that he would always protect the Prophet ﷺ

Assessment from the Quraysh and the Jews

The Quraysh's next attempt was in the form of academic assessment and questioning

Quraysh sent Nadhr ibn Harith and ''Uqbah ibn Abi Mu'eet to Yathrib (Madinah)

Question 1: People of the Cave

Question 2: The Man who Traversed the Earth

Question 3: The Soul's Nature

Pause in the Revelation

Hostility of the Quraysh

With no success, the Quraysh became increasingly hostile.

Quraysh tried to dissuade pilgrims from listening to the Prophet ﷺ.

Quraysh approach Abu Talib Again

- Quraysh offer a trade for the Prophet ﷺ

The Quraysh questioned why the Quran was not revealed to someone more honorable from their society.

Hostility of the Quraysh

Al-'Aas ibn Wa'il would mock the Prophet ﷺ due to all of his sons passing away.

- He would chant: بتر محمد
    - This means: "Muhammad has been cut off" meaning his name will not continue

Allah SWT revealed Surah Al-Kawthar in response to Al'Aas ibn Wa'il

بِسۡمِ اللّٰهِ الرَّحۡمٰنِ الرَّحِيۡمِ

اِنَّاۤ اَعۡطَيۡنٰكَ الۡكَوۡثَرَ ﴿۱﴾ فَصَلِّ لِرَبِّكَ وَانۡحَرۡ ﴿۲﴾ اِنَّ شَانِئَكَ هُوَ الۡاَبۡتَرُ ﴿۳﴾

(O Prophet,) surely We have given to you Al-Kauthar(1) So, offer Salah (prayer) to your Lord, and sacrifice(2) Surely it is your enemy whose traces are cut off(3) [108:1-3]

The Wisdoms of Losing His Sons:

Persecution of Muslims

Violent persecution began to become common in the 4th year of Prophethood.

The Family of Yasir

- Abu Jahl forced Ammar to insult the Prophet ﷺ

Mus'ab ibn Umair (RA)

Bilal ibn Rabah (RA)

Persecution of Muslims

Khabbab ibn al-Aratt (RA)

Suhaib ibn Sinan (ar-Rumi) (RA)

Zanirah (RA)

Enemies of the Prophet ﷺ

Abu Lahab

Abu Jahl

'Uqbah ibn Abi Mu'eet

Ubayy ibn Khalaf

Quraysh's Tactics Against the Prophet ﷺ

The Prophet ﷺ was assaulted while preaching Islam in the marketplace.

The Quraysh would attempt to assassinate the Prophet .ﷺ

- Abu Bakr's (RA) protection

The Quraysh placed the intestines of a camel on his ﷺ back as he prayed.

Migration to Abyssinia

First Migration:

Second Migration:

Reasons for Choosing Abyssinia

The Quraysh sent ‘Amr ibn al-’Aas and Abdullah ibn Abi Rabi’ah to bring those who migrated back to Mecca.

Conversion of Negus نجاشي

.

.

Hamza's (RA) Conversion

While walking to Mount Safa, Abu Jahl began saying vile things to the Messenger ﷺ

Abdullah ibn Jud'an's slave witnessed this and informed Hamza (RA)

Hamza's (RA) Response:

Negotiations of Quraysh

Quraysh tried to bribe the Prophet ﷺ so he would stop spreading the message

The Prophet ﷺ refused anything they offered him

'Utbah ibn Rabiah offers a bribe

Negotiations of Quraysh

46

The Prophet ﷺ responds with the Quran

بِسْمِ اللهِ الرَّحْمٰنِ الرَّحِيْمِ

حٰمٓ ﴿١﴾ تَنْزِيْلٌ مِّنَ الرَّحْمٰنِ الرَّحِيْمِ ﴿٢﴾ كِتٰبٌ فُصِّلَتْ اٰيٰتُهٗ قُرْاٰنًا عَرَبِيًّا لِّقَوْمٍ
يَّعْلَمُوْنَ ﴿٣﴾ بَشِيْرًا وَّ نَذِيْرًا فَاَعْرَضَ اَكْثَرُهُمْ فَهُمْ لَا يَسْمَعُوْنَ ﴿٤﴾ وَ قَالُوْا
قُلُوْبُنَا فِيْٓ اَكِنَّةٍ مِّمَّا تَدْعُوْنَآ اِلَيْهِ وَ فِيْٓ اٰذَانِنَا وَقْرٌ وَّ مِنْۢ بَيْنِنَا وَ بَيْنِكَ حِجَابٌ
فَاعْمَلْ اِنَّنَا عٰمِلُوْنَ ﴿٥﴾ قُلْ اِنَّمَآ اَنَا بَشَرٌ مِّثْلُكُمْ يُوْحٰٓى اِلَيَّ اَنَّمَآ اِلٰهُكُمْ اِلٰهٌ
وَّاحِدٌ فَاسْتَقِيْمُوْٓا اِلَيْهِ وَ اسْتَغْفِرُوْهُ وَ وَيْلٌ لِّلْمُشْرِكِيْنَ ﴿٦﴾ الَّذِيْنَ لَا يُؤْتُوْنَ الزَّكٰوةَ
وَ هُمْ بِالْاٰخِرَةِ هُمْ كٰفِرُوْنَ ﴿٧﴾ اِنَّ الَّذِيْنَ اٰمَنُوْا وَ عَمِلُوا الصّٰلِحٰتِ لَهُمْ اَجْرٌ غَيْرُ
مَمْنُوْنٍ ﴿٨﴾ قُلْ اَئِنَّكُمْ لَتَكْفُرُوْنَ بِالَّذِيْ خَلَقَ الْاَرْضَ فِيْ يَوْمَيْنِ وَ تَجْعَلُوْنَ لَهٗٓ
اَنْدَادًا ذٰلِكَ رَبُّ الْعٰلَمِيْنَ ﴿٩﴾ وَ جَعَلَ فِيْهَا رَوَاسِيَ مِنْ فَوْقِهَا وَ بٰرَكَ فِيْهَا وَ قَدَّرَ
فِيْهَآ اَقْوَاتَهَا فِيْٓ اَرْبَعَةِ اَيَّامٍ سَوَآءً لِّلسَّآئِلِيْنَ ﴿١٠﴾ ثُمَّ اسْتَوٰٓى اِلَى السَّمَآءِ وَ هِيَ
دُخَانٌ فَقَالَ لَهَا وَ لِلْاَرْضِ ائْتِيَا طَوْعًا اَوْ كَرْهًا قَالَتَآ اَتَيْنَا طَآئِعِيْنَ ﴿١١﴾ فَقَضٰهُنَّ
سَبْعَ سَمٰوَاتٍ فِيْ يَوْمَيْنِ وَ اَوْحٰى فِيْ كُلِّ سَمَآءٍ اَمْرَهَا وَ زَيَّنَّا السَّمَآءَ الدُّنْيَا بِمَصَابِيْحَ
وَ حِفْظًا ذٰلِكَ تَقْدِيْرُ الْعَزِيْزِ الْعَلِيْمِ ﴿١٢﴾ فَاِنْ اَعْرَضُوْا فَقُلْ اَنْذَرْتُكُمْ صٰعِقَةً
مِّثْلَ صٰعِقَةِ عَادٍ وَّ ثَمُوْدَ ﴿١٣﴾

Ha Meem (1) A Revelation from (Allah), Most Gracious, Most Merciful (2) A Book, whereof the verses are explained in detail;- a Quran in Arabic, for people who understand (3) Giving good news and admonition: yet most of them turn away, and so they hear not (4) They say: "Our hearts are under veils, (concealed) from that to which thou dost invite us, and in our ears in a deafness, and between us and thee is a screen: so do thou (what thou wilt); for us, we shall do (what we will!)" (5) Say thou: "I am but a man like you: It is revealed to me by Inspiration, that your Allah is one Allah. so stand true to Him, and ask for His Forgiveness." And woe to those who join gods with Allah, (6) Those who practice not regular Charity, and who even deny the Hereafter. (7) For those who believe and work deeds of righteousness is a reward that will never fail (8) Say: Is it that ye deny Him Who created the earth in two Days? And do ye join equals with Him? He is the Lord of (all) the Worlds. (9) He set on the (earth), mountains standing firm, high above it, and bestowed blessings on the earth, and measure therein all things to give them nourishment in due proportion, in four Days, in accordance with (the needs of) those who seek (Sustenance) (10) Moreover He comprehended in His design the sky, and it had been (as) smoke: He said to it and to the earth: "Come ye together, willingly or unwillingly." They said: "We do come (together), in willing obedience." (11) So He completed them as seven firmaments in two Days, and He assigned to each heaven its duty and command. And We adorned the lower heaven with lights, and (provided it) with guard. Such is the Decree of (Him) the Exalted in Might, Full of Knowledge. (12) But if they turn away, say thou: "I have warned you of a stunning Punishment (as of thunder and lightning) like that which (overtook) the 'Ad and the Thamud!" (13) [41:1-13]

Umar ibn al-Khattab's (RA) Conversion

The Prophet ﷺ would often make du'a for the guidance of 'Umar (RA) and Abu Jahl

On his way to assassinate the Prophet ﷺ,'Umar (RA) was stopped by Nu'aym ibn Abdullah (RA)

'Umar's detour to the house of Fatima bint Al-Khattab and husband Sa'eed ibn Zaid (RA)

- Khabbab ibn Al-Arat (RA)

- Umar's (RA) Heart Softens

Umar ibn al-Khattab's (RA) Conversion

"What magnificent and gracious words!"

إِنَّنِيٓ أَنَا ٱللَّهُ لَآ إِلَٰهَ إِلَّآ أَنَا۠ فَٱعۡبُدۡنِي وَأَقِمِ ٱلصَّلَوٰةَ لِذِكۡرِيٓ ﴿١٤﴾

Certainly I am Allah! There is no other being worthy of worship but Me. So worship Me and establish Salah for My remembrance. [20:14]

'Umar (RA) was blown away by the Quran and asked Khabbab (RA) to take him to the Prophet ﷺ

The Prophet ﷺ invites 'Umar (RA) to Islam

Impact of 'Umar's (RA) conversion

Given the title Al-Farooq by the Prophet ﷺ

Phase Review Questions

1. What were the events that preceded revelation?

2. Where would the Prophet ﷺ go to isolate himself, and what would he do there?

3. What were the first verses revealed to the Prophet ﷺ.

4. What was his ﷺ reaction?

5. How did Khadijah (RA) respond?

6. Who was the first convert to Islam?

7. Why was the call to Islam quiet at first?

8. Where was the first gathering place for the Muslims?

Phase Review Questions

9. List some of the tribes outside of Mecca that began accepting Islam:

10. List three enemies of Islam who were moved by the Quran:

11. What were the three phases of the Quraysh's attack on Islam?

12. What were some things they offered the Prophet ﷺ?

13. What were some questions they tested him ﷺ with?

14. Which of the companions were most heavily persecuted?

15. What caused the migration to Abyssinia?

16. What was the name of the leader of Abyssinia?

Phase Review Questions

17. What led Hamza (RA) to accept Islam?

18. How many days after Hamza (RA) did ‘Umar (RA) accept Islam?

19. What surah did ‘Umar (RA) hear being recited?

20. What was the name of ‘Umar’s sister (RA)?

21. Who taught ‘Umar’s (RA) sister and her husband Quran?

22. What did the Prophet ﷺ name Umar (RA)?

LATE MECCA

A period in which the torment of the Muslims increased, the spread of Islam was very limited, and the believers began planning to leave Mecca.

LATE MECCA

- Prophethood Map
- The Boycott
- The Year of Sorrow
- The Journey to Ta'if
- Al-Isra'
- Al-Mi'raj
- Wisdoms of Mi'raj
- Return from Mi'raj
- The First Pledge of 'Aqabah
- The Second Pledge of 'Aqabah
- Meccan Phase Overview
- Phase Review Questions

Prophethood Map

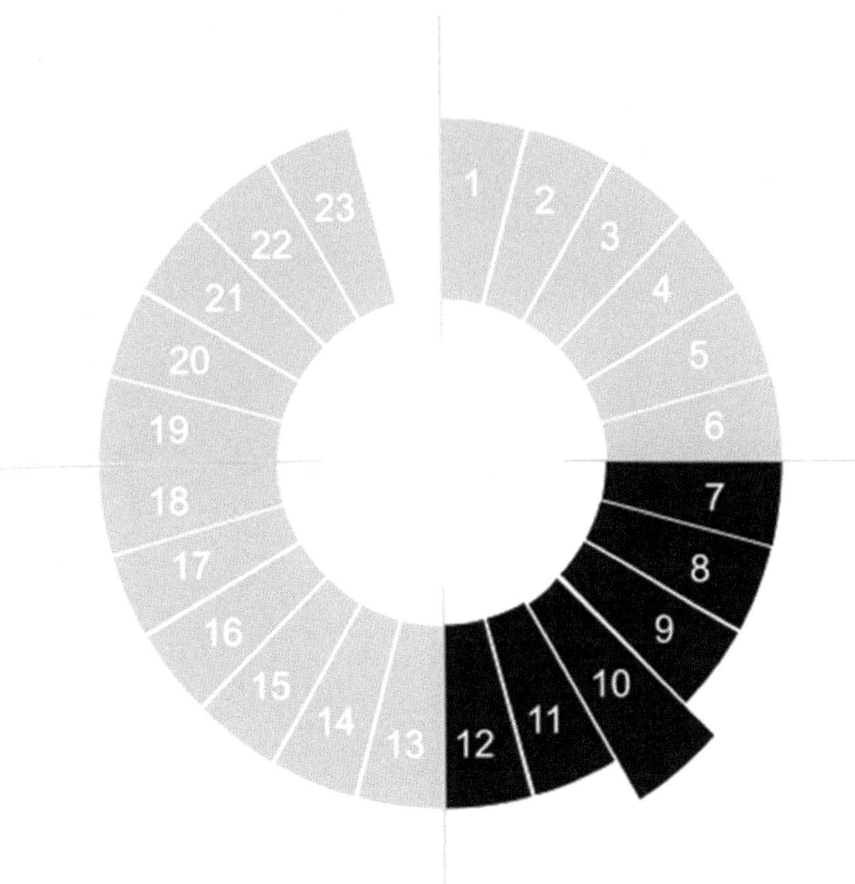

The Boycott of Banu Hashim

The Quraysh impose a difficult three-year socio-economic boycott on Prophet's ﷺ clan, Banu Hashim.

The Year of Sadness

This is a long year for the Prophet ﷺ; he lost his wife and uncle, and was persecuted by the people of Ta'if.

Isra' and Mi'raj

In a single night, the Prophet ﷺ took a miraculous journey to Jerusalem before ascending up to the heavens.

First Pledge of 'Aqabah

Twelve pilgrims pledged to protect and obey the Prophet ﷺ

The Boycott

The Growth of Islam

Banu Hashim and Banu Al-Muttalib are boycotted

Mansoor ibn 'Ikramah wrote the agreement

Banu Hashim and Banu Al-Muttalib moved to the outskirts of Mecca, into the valley of Abu Talib

- Abdullah ibn Abbas was born during this time

Five people from Quraysh lobbied for the boycott to be lifted:

- Hisham ibn 'Amr
- Mut'im ibn 'Adi
- Abul-Bakhtar
- Zam'ah ibn Al-Aswad
- Zuhair ibn Umayyah

The Quraysh Agree to Lift the Boycott

Upon entering the Ka'bah to remove the treaty, they find that it had all been destroyed except for the name of Allah SWT

The Year of Sorrow

This was the 10th year of prophethood, and it was among the most difficult times in the Prophet's ﷺ life

- The Death of Abu Talib

- Abu Talib refused to utter the Shahadah despite the Prophet ﷺ pleading with him

- The Prophet ﷺ pledged that he would continue to make du'a of forgiveness for him

    - Allah SWT revealed verses :

مَا كَانَ لِلنَّبِيِّ وَ الَّذِينَ اٰمَنُوٓا اَنْ يَّسْتَغْفِرُوْا لِلْمُشْرِكِيْنَ وَ لَوْ كَانُوٓا اُولِيْ قُرْبٰى مِنْۢ بَعْدِ مَا
تَبَيَّنَ لَهُمْ اَنَّهُمْ اَصْحٰبُ الْجَحِيْمِ ﴿١١٣﴾

It is not (permissible) for the Prophet and the believers to seek forgiveness for the Mushrikin, even if they are kinsmen, after it became clear to them that they are the people of hell [9:113]

اِنَّكَ لَا تَهْدِيْ مَنْ اَحْبَبْتَ وَ لٰكِنَّ اللّٰهَ يَهْدِيْ مَنْ يَّشَآءُ ۚ وَ هُوَ اَعْلَمُ بِالْمُهْتَدِيْنَ ﴿٥٦﴾

You cannot give guidance to whomsoever you wish, but Allah gives guidance to whomsoever He will, and He best knows the ones who are on the right path [28:56]

- Abu Bakr (RA) sought the Prophet's ﷺ permission to migrate to Abyssinia.

The Year of Sorrow

The Death of Khadijah (RA)

Jibreel came down to give her glad tidings and greetings from her Lord

Journey to Ta'if

50

The Prophet ﷺ went to Ta'if with Zaid ibn Haritha to find a place the Muslims would be protected

Presenting Islam to the Chiefs

- 'Abdiyaalil

- Mas'ood

- Habib

Response of Ta'if

Journey to Ta'if

The Prophet ﷺ sought refuge in the garden of 'Utbah and Shaybah

In this time of distress the Prophet ﷺ made du'a:

اَللّٰهُمَّ اِلَیْکَ اَشْکُوْا ضُعْفَ قُوَّتِیْ وَ قِلَّةَ حِیْلَتِیْ وَ هَوَانِیْ عَلَی النَّاسِ یَآاَرْحَمَ الَّراحِمِیْنَ،
اَنْتَ رَبُّ الْمُسْتَضْعَفِیْنَ اِلٰی مَنْ تَکِلُنِیْ اِلٰی عَدُوٍّ بَعِیْدٍ یَّتَجَهَّمُنِیْ اَمْ اِلٰی صَدِیْقٍ قَرِیْبٍ
مَّلَّکْتَهٗ اَمْرِیْ اِنْ لَّمْ تَکُنْ بِکَ غَضَبَانًا عَلَیَّ فَلَآ اُبَالِیْ غَیْرَ اَنْ عَافِیَتُکَ، اَوْسَعُ لِیْ اَعُوْذُ
بِنُوْرِوَجْهِکَ الَّذِیْ اَشْرَقَتْ لَهُ الظُّلُمَاتُ وَصَلَحَ عَلَیْهِ اَمْرُالدُّنْیَاوَالْاٰخِرَةِ مِنْ اَنْ تُنَزِّلَ بِیْ
غَضَبَکَ اَوْ یَحِلَّ بِیْ سَخَطُکَ وَلَکَ الْعَتْبٰی حَتّٰی تَرْضٰی وَلَا حَوْلَ وَلَا قُوَّةَ اِلَّابِکَ

O Allah! Only to You do I complain of my infirmity, my inadequate strategies and of my humiliation before the people. O most merciful of the merciful! You are the Lord of the weak and helpless. To whom do You consign me? Would You condemn me to an impolite and ill-tempered enemy who will enrage me or would You consign me to a close friend to whom You would entrust my affairs? If You are not angry with me, I am not concerned in the least but Your protection and safety is more accommodating and pleasant to me. I seek refuge with the Noor (radiance) of Your being that has brightened the darkness and the radiance upon which the affairs of this world and the hereafter depend, with the medium of this radiance I seek Your refuge, O Allah, from Your wrath descending upon me or from Your fury being unleashed over me. And only to You (do I wish to express my lamentations) until You are content. There is no power (to repel evil) nor might (to do good) but only that which You have decreed. [Tabarani]

Journey to Ta'if

The angel makes an offer

Addas accepts Islam

Jinn also accept Islam

Mut'im ibn 'Adi

Al-Isra'

سُبْحَانَ الَّذِى أَسْرَىٰ بِعَبْدِهِ لَيْلًا مِّنَ الْمَسْجِدِ الْحَرَامِ إِلَى الْمَسْجِدِ الْأَقْصَى الَّذِى بَارَكْنَا
حَوْلَهُ لِنُرِيَهُ مِنْ آيَاتِنَا ۚ إِنَّهُ هُوَ السَّمِيعُ الْبَصِيرُ ﴿١﴾

Glorious is He Who made his servant travel by night from Al-Masjid-ul-Haram to Al-Masjid-ul-Aqsa whose environs We have blessed, so that We let him see some of Our signs. Surely, He is the All-Hearing, the All-Seeing [17:1]

The Night Journey from Mecca to Jerusalem took place after the most difficult time in the Prophet's ﷺ life.

The Prophet ﷺ was asleep in the home of Umm Hani when Jibril woke him up.

The Splitting of the Prophet's ﷺ Chest

Buraq

Al-Isra'

The Prophet ﷺ witnessed many different scenes on the way to Jerusalem:

- Voices called out to the Prophet ﷺ
- There was an old woman on the side of the road
- The Dajjal
- People were scratching their faces with copper nails
- There were people swimming in a river and swallowing stones
- The people whose heads were being crushed by boulders
- He ﷺ saw people eat rotten food despite the fresh food in front of them
- The Prophet ﷺ smelled a beautiful fragrance

Prayer in Jerusalem

Al-Mi'raj

After leading the Prophets in prayer he was lifted up through the heavens and encountered many Prophets:

1st heaven: Prophet Adam (AS)

2nd heaven: Prophet Yahya and Isa (AS)

3rd heaven: Prophet Yusuf (AS)

4th heaven: Prophet Idris (AS)

5th heaven: Prophet Harun (AS)

6th heaven: Prophet Musa (AS)

7th heaven: Prophet Ibrahim (AS)

- Ibrahim (AS) was resting against Al-Bait Al-Ma'moor

Al-Mi'raj

Sidratul Muntaha and Jibreel

Ascension to Dharif Al-Aqlam

Prophet Muhammad ﷺ in the Presence of Allah SWT

Three Gifts from Allah SWT

Wisdoms of Al-Mi'raj

Why didn't Ibrahim (AS) tell the Prophet ﷺ to lessen the amount of prayers?

When the Prophet ﷺ met Allah SWT, all his titles were left behind and he was known only as a slave of Allah.

The Prophet ﷺ was taken up during the night, not the day.

Every Prophet that the Prophet W met in the skies had a significance.

He W witnessed the angels worshipping Allah SWT in only one position

Return from Al-Mi'raj

n the morning, the Prophet Muhammad ﷺ informed the Quraysh about his Night Journey

The Response of the Quraysh

Abu Bakr (RA) Named Al-Siddiq

Features of Baitul Maqdis

The Caravans

The Believer's Ascension

The First Pledge of 'Aqabah

52

The Prophet ﷺ called pilgrims to Islam during the days of Hajj.

In the 11th year of Prophethood, a group of six pilgrims from Yathrib (Madinah) come to Mecca.

- As'ad ibn Zurārah, 'Awf ibn al-Hārith, Rāfi' ibn Mālik, Qutbah ibn 'Āmir, 'Uqbah ibn 'Āmir, and Jābir ibn 'Abdullah

The First Pledge of 'Aqabah

- Terms of the pledge: We will not worship any one but one Allah; we will not steal; neither will we commit adultery, nor kill our children; we will not utter slander, intentionally forging falsehood and we will not disobey you in any just matter.

Mus'ab ibn Umair (RA) was sent to Yathrib to give Da'wah and teach its people about Islam.

- Sa'd ibn Mu'adh & Usayd ibn Hudair (RA) accepted Islam

The Second Pledge of 'Aqabah

Mus'ab (RA) returned the following year (13th) with 73 men and two women from Yathrib to pledge allegiance once again.

This time, they pledged their lives to the Prophet ﷺ.

Bukhari and Muslim report that Ka'ab ibn Malik (RA) said:

"I would not trade my attendance of this pledge for the attendance of Badr, despite Badr being more well known to the people."

These pledges paved the path for the Hijrah to take place.

Meccan Phase Overview

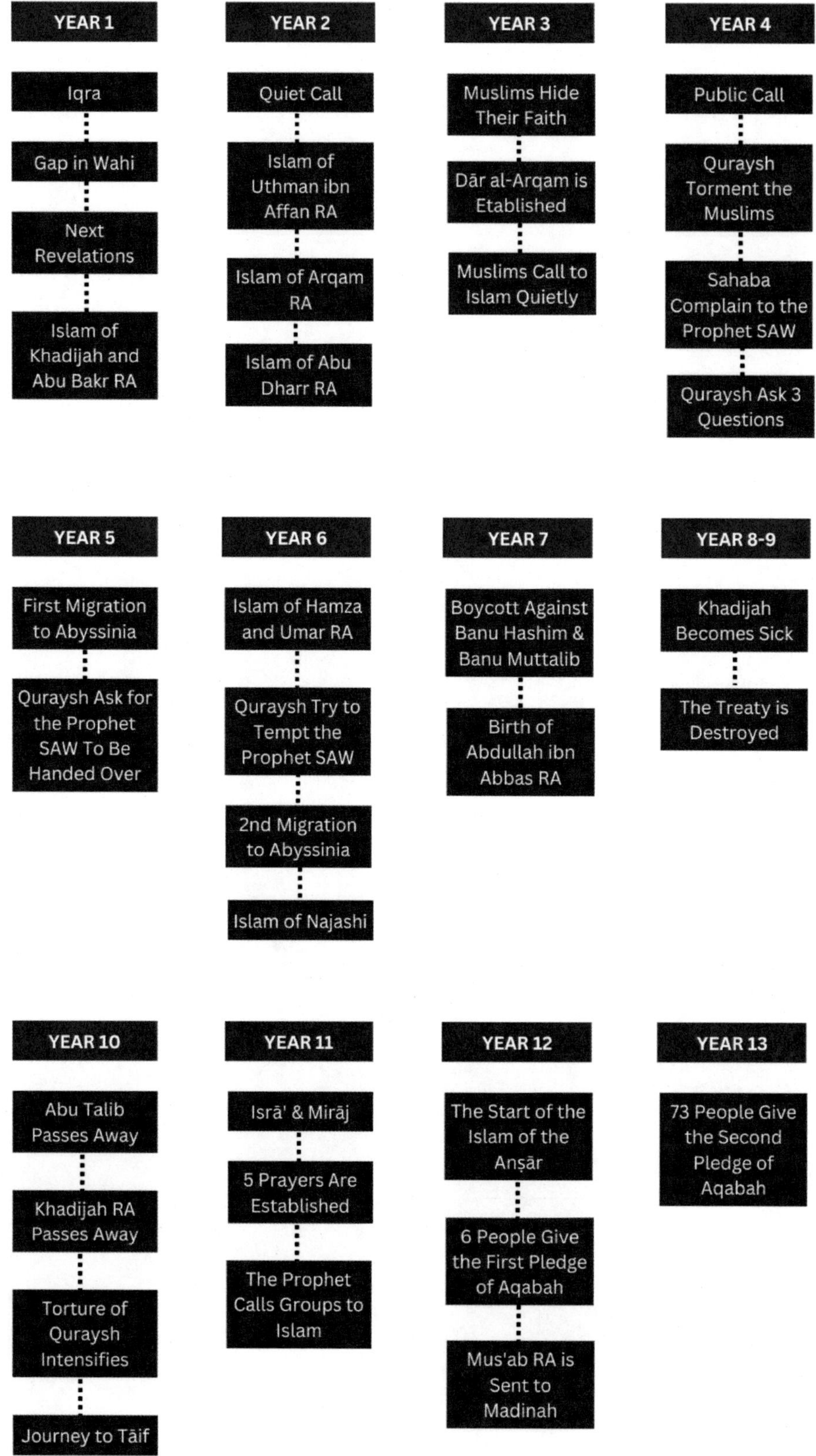
YEAR 1
Iqra
Gap in Wahi
Next Revelations
Islam of Khadijah and Abu Bakr RA
YEAR 2
Quiet Call
Islam of Uthman ibn Affan RA
Islam of Arqam RA
Islam of Abu Dharr RA
YEAR 3
Muslims Hide Their Faith
Dār al-Arqam is Etablished
Muslims Call to Islam Quietly
YEAR 4
Public Call
Quraysh Torment the Muslims
Sahaba Complain to the Prophet SAW
Quraysh Ask 3 Questions
YEAR 5
First Migration to Abyssinia
Quraysh Ask for the Prophet SAW To Be Handed Over
YEAR 6
Islam of Hamza and Umar RA
Quraysh Try to Tempt the Prophet SAW
2nd Migration to Abyssinia
Islam of Najashi
YEAR 7
Boycott Against Banu Hashim & Banu Muttalib
Birth of Abdullah ibn Abbas RA
YEAR 8-9
Khadijah Becomes Sick
The Treaty is Destroyed
YEAR 10
Abu Talib Passes Away
Khadijah RA Passes Away
Torture of Quraysh Intensifies
Journey to Tāif
YEAR 11
Isrā' & Mirāj
5 Prayers Are Established
The Prophet Calls Groups to Islam
YEAR 12
The Start of the Islam of the Anṣār
6 People Give the First Pledge of Aqabah
Mus'ab RA is Sent to Madinah
YEAR 13
73 People Give the Second Pledge of Aqabah

Phase Review Questions

1. How many years of isolation did Banu Hashim and Banu Muttalib live in?

2. Who wrote the agreement? What was his punishment?

3. How was the agreement destroyed?

4. What is the lesson from the death of Abu Talib?

5. At what age did Khadijah (RA) pass away? How long was she married to the Prophet ﷺ ?

6. Why did the Prophet ﷺ go to Ta'if?

7. Who were the three chiefs?

8. Why did the Prophet ﷺ refuse to crush the people of Ta'if?

Phase Review Questions

9. Whose protection did the Prophet ﷺ return with from Ta'if?

10. What is one lesson you take from the Year of Sorrow?

11. After waking him up for the night journey, where did Jibreel take the Prophet ﷺ ?

12. What did the Prophet ﷺ ride to Jerusalem?

13. Why was this journey a relief to the Prophet ﷺ ?

14. How many prayers were initially assigned to Muslims by Allah SWT?

15. What is Dharif Al-Aqlam?

16. How many people were at the First Pledge of 'Aqabah and how many were at the Second Pledge?

17. Who was sent to Yathrib to teach Islam?

18. Why were these pledges so important?

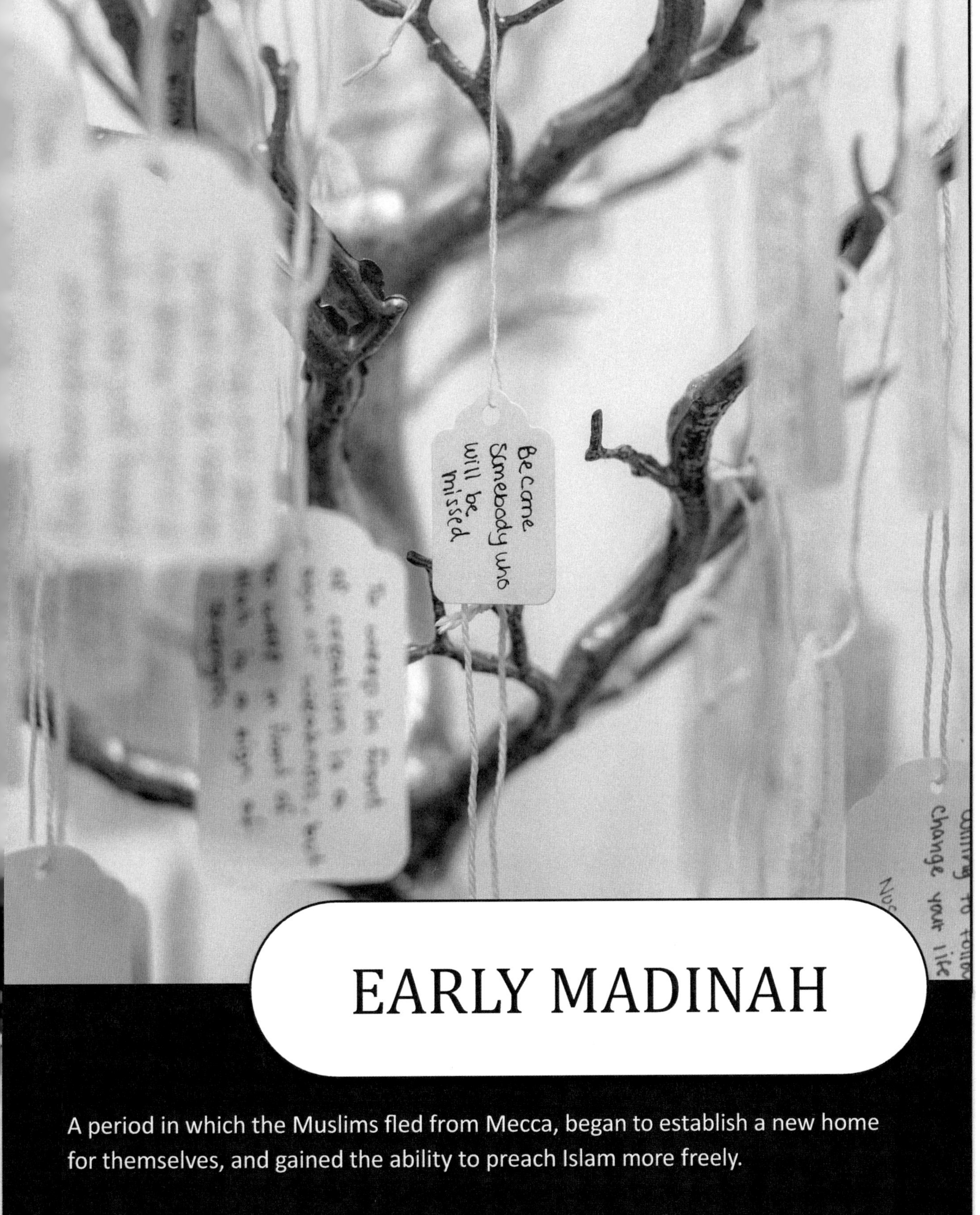

EARLY MADINAH

A period in which the Muslims fled from Mecca, began to establish a new home for themselves, and gained the ability to preach Islam more freely.

EARLY MADINAH

- Prophethood Map
- Hijrah of the Companions
- Assassination Plot of the Prophet ﷺ
- Hijrah of the Prophet ﷺ
- Cave of Thawr
- Umm Ma'bad
- Masjid Quba
- The First Jumu'ah
- Entry into Madinah
- Rabbis and the Prophet ﷺ
- House of Abu Ayyub
- Islam of Salman Al-Farisi
- Brotherhood
- Acclimation to Madinah
- Virtues of Madinah
- Construction of Masjid An-Nabawi
- Housing for the Prophet and His Wives ﷺ
- Ashaab al-Suffa

EARLY MADINAH

- Treaty with the Jewish Tribes
- Inception of Adhan
- The Water of Madinah
- Marriage with 'Aisha (RA)
- Virtues of 'Aisha (RA)
- Change of Qiblah
- Ramadan, Eid, and Zakat are Legislated
- Military Expeditions
- Events that Led to Badr
- Before the Battle
- The Battle of Badr
- Aftermath of the Battle of Badr
- Madinah After the Battle of Badr
- Events Leading to Uhud
- The Battle of Uhud
- Death of Hamzah (RA) and Mus'ab (RA)
- Companions in Uhud
- Aftermath of the Battle of Uhud

EARLY MADINAH

- Lessons from the Battle of Uhud
- Events of 3 A.H.
- Incident of Raji'
- Bi'r Ma'unah
- Battle of Banu Nadheer
- Prohibition of Liquor
- The Expedition of Dhaat ur Riqaa'
- The Expedition of Banu Mustaliq
- Incident of Slander
- Battle of Khandaq
- The Expulsion of Banu Quraydha
- Events After the Expulsion
- Year of Expeditions
- Phase Review Questions

Prophethood Map

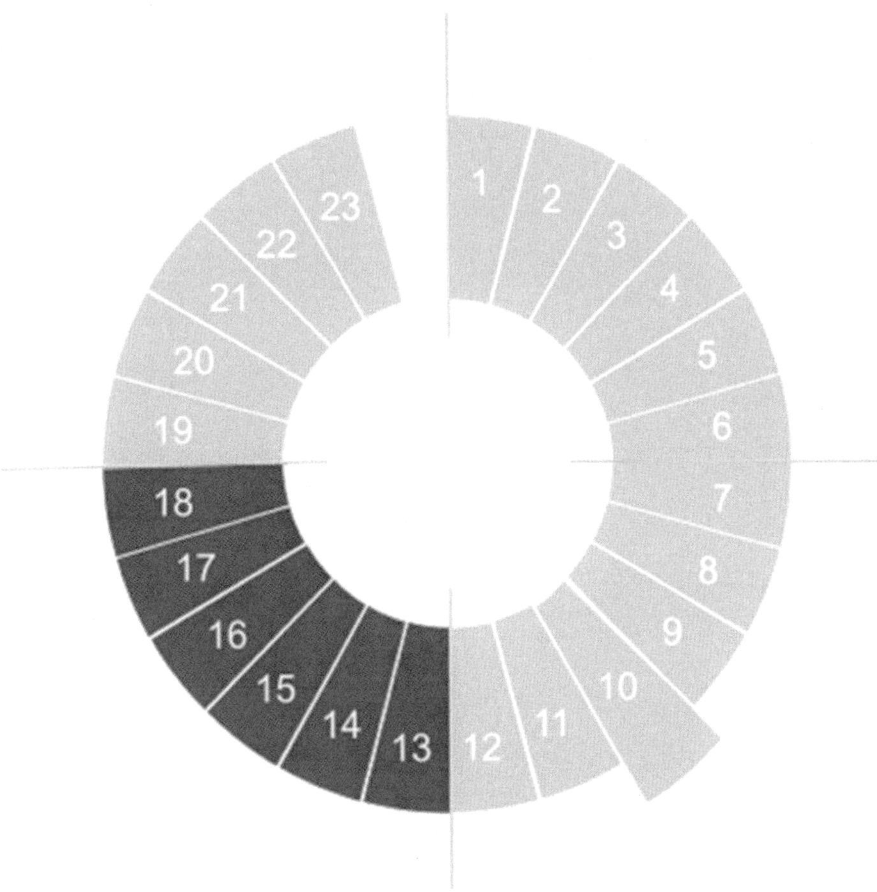

Hijrah
The Prophet ﷺ migrates to Madinah and begins building a new community.

Raids
This is a year of caravan raids directed against the Quraysh.

Battle of Badr
Being outnumbered, the Muslims march to Badr and pull off a stunning victory against the Quraysh.

Battle of Uhud
The Quraysh march north of Madinah and inflict serious damage to the Muslim army.

Alcohol Prohibition
The final verses revealed for alcohol prohibition.

Battle of the Trench
The Quraysh and their allies converge on Madinah, laying siege to the city, but return home defeated.

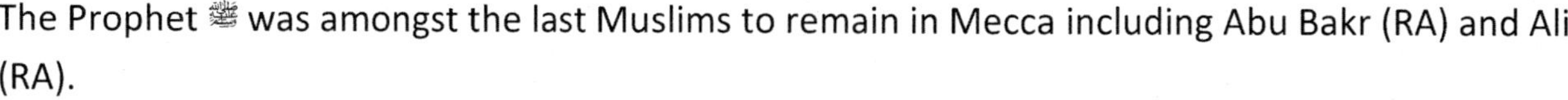

Hijrah of the Companions

The Prophet ﷺ was amongst the last Muslims to remain in Mecca including Abu Bakr (RA) and Ali (RA).

The Prophet ﷺ now gave permission for the companions to begin to migrate.

- Umm Salamah (RA)

- Suhaib Al-Rumi (RA)

  - Allah SWT mentioned his sacrifice in the Quran

وَ مِنَ النَّاسِ مَنۡ يَّشۡرِىۡ نَفۡسَهُ ابۡتِغَآءَ مَرۡضَاتِ اللّٰهِ ۔وَ اللّٰهُ رَءُوۡفٌۢ بِالۡعِبَادِ ﴿٢٠٧﴾

And of the people is he who sells himself, seeking means to the approval of Allah and Allah is kind to [His] servants [2:207]

- Umar (RA)

- Bani Jash

- Salim Mawla Abi Hudhaifa

Assassination Plot of the Prophet ﷺ

Allah SWT grants the Prophet ﷺ permission to migrate

- Abu Bakr (RA) asks the Prophet ﷺ if he could join him

Quraysh assembles to plot the assassination of the Prophet ﷺ

- Iblees Joins the Gathering with Meccans

- Allah SWT informs the Prophet ﷺ through Jibreel

وَ اِذْ يَمْكُرُ بِكَ الَّذِيْنَ كَفَرُوْا لِيُثْبِتُوْكَ اَوْ يَقْتُلُوْكَ اَوْ يُخْرِجُوْكَ ۚ وَ يَمْكُرُوْنَ وَ يَمْكُرُ اللّٰهُ ۚ

وَ اللّٰهُ خَيْرُ الْمٰكِرِيْنَ ﴿٣٠﴾

And (recall) when the disbelievers were conspiring against you to hold you as a captive, or to kill you or to expel you. They were planning, and Allah was planning, Allah is the best planner [8:30]

Assassination Plot of the Prophet ﷺ

Abu Bakr (RA) Prepares for Travel

The Quraysh arrive at the House of the Prophet ﷺ during the night

The Prophet ﷺ Recites Verses for Protection and Escapes

وَ جَعَلْنَا مِنْۢ بَيْنِ اَيْدِيْهِمْ سَدًّا وَّ مِنْ خَلْفِهِمْ سَدًّا فَاَغْشَيْنٰهُمْ فَهُمْ لَا يُبْصِرُوْنَ ﴿٩﴾

And We have placed a barrier in from of them and a barrier behind them, and (thus) they are encircled by Us; so they do not see (36:9)

Hijrah of the Prophet ﷺ

When they left Mecca, the Prophet ﷺ turned to the city and said:

عَنْ اَبِى هُرَيْرَة رَضِىَ اللهُ عَنْهُ، أَنَّ النَّبِيَّ ﷺ وَقَفَ عَلَى الْحَزْوَرَةِ فَقَال - عَلِمْتُ اَنَّكِ خَيْرُ اَرْضِ اللهِ وَ اَحَبُّ اَرْضِ اللهِ، وَلَوْلَا اَنَّ اَهْلَكِ اَخْرَجُوْنِى مِنْكِ مَا خَرَجْتُ

"I know that you are the best place on the earth, and the most beloved place to Allah and if your people did not remove me I would have not left you." [Bayhaqi-Dalail]

Abdullah ibn Uraiqit

- The Hired Guide

Cave of Thawr

Detour South to the Cave of Thawr

Abu Bakr Gets Stung

Miracles of the Cave

إِلَّا تَنصُرُوهُ فَقَدْ نَصَرَهُ اللَّهُ إِذْ أَخْرَجَهُ الَّذِينَ كَفَرُوا ثَانِيَ اثْنَيْنِ إِذْ هُمَا فِي الْغَارِ إِذْ يَقُولُ
لِصَاحِبِهِ لَا تَحْزَنْ إِنَّ اللَّهَ مَعَنَا ۖ فَأَنزَلَ اللَّهُ سَكِينَتَهُ عَلَيْهِ وَأَيَّدَهُ بِجُنُودٍ لَّمْ تَرَوْهَا
وَجَعَلَ كَلِمَةَ الَّذِينَ كَفَرُوا السُّفْلَىٰ ۗ وَكَلِمَةُ اللَّهِ هِيَ الْعُلْيَا ۗ وَاللَّهُ عَزِيزٌ حَكِيمٌ

If you do not aid the Prophet - Allah has already aided him when those who disbelieved had driven him out [of Mecca] as one of two, when they were in the cave and he said to his companion, "Do not grieve; indeed Allah is with us." And Allah sent down his tranquility upon him and supported him with angels you did not see and made the word of those who disbelieved the lowest, while the word of Allah that is the highest. And Allah is Exalted in Might and Wise. [9:40]

Cave of Thawr

Abu Bakr's (RA) Children Help

Bounty Placed on the Prophet ﷺ

Journey to Madinah Begins in Rabi' Al-Awwal

Suraqah ibn Malik

Umm Ma'bad

Tent of Umm Ma'bad

- The Prophet ﷺ and Abu Bakr (RA) stopped at her tent for food, but she had nothing.

- He ﷺ milked an animal which had no milk.

- She gave the best physical description of the Prophet ﷺ .

Umm Ma'bad

1. A man with obvious beauty and cleanliness,
2. a glowing countenance,
3. and a good appearance/disposition;
4. with no bulging stomach disgracing him,
5. or a small head disparaging him;
6. is overtly handsome
7. and wholly beautiful;
8. his eyes are wide and very white and black
9. and eyelashes are long;
10. whose voice is devoid of hoarseness,
11. neck is long,
12. and beard is full;
13. the white part of whose eyes is extremely white, and the black part of whose eyes is extremely black,
14. as if his eyelids have kohl naturally;
15. whose eyebrows arch longitudinally and thinly
16. (as if they) meet;
17. who has an extremely black hair;
18. who is stately when silent
19. and is gorgeous when speaking;
20. who is the most beautiful and striking man from far and the best and most beautiful from close;
21. whose speech is sweet, clear, and decisive,
22. neither vaguely short, nor boringly and pointlessly long;
23. whose words flow forth like a perfect string of pearls;
24. of medium height
25. that neither elicits contempt to avert him for shortness, nor aversion to him for excessive tallness;
26. who is a branch between two branches ; he is the most radiant of the three and the most well-respected;
27. whose companions surround him; when he speaks they listen attentively to his speech, and when he commands they vie with each other to fulfill his commands.
28. who is well served and attended,
29. who is neither a scowler
30. nor a prattler.

1. رجلٌ ظَاهِرُ الْوَضَاءَةِ (الحُسن والنظافة)
2. أَبْلَجُ الْوَجْهِ (مُشرقُ الوجهِ مُضيئُه)
3. حَسَنُ الْخَلْقِ/الخُلُق
4. لَمْ تَعِبْهُ ثُجْلَةٌ (عِظَمُ البطن مع استرخاء أسفله)
5. وَلَمْ تزرِ بِهِ صَعْلَةٌ (صِغَرُ الرأس)
6. وَسِيمٌ (المشهور بالحُسن كأنه صار الحُسن له سمة)
7. قَسِيمٌ (كل موضع منه أخذ قسما من الجمال)
8. فِي عَيْنَيْهِ دَعَجٌ (اشتد سوادها وبياضها واتسعت)
9. وَفِي أَشْفَارِهِ وَطَفٌ (طُول)
10. وَفِي صوتِهِ صَحَلٌ (شبه البُحَّة)
11. وَفِي عُنُقِهِ سَطَعٌ (طولُ العُنُقِ وارتفاعُه)
12. وَفِي لِحْيَتِهِ كَثَاثَةٌ (كثافة)
13. أَحْوَرُ (اشتد بياض بياض عينيه مع سواد سوادهما)
14. أَكْحَلُ (ذو كُحْلٍ، اسودت أجفانه خلقة)
15. أَزَجّ (مُقوَّسُ الحاجبين طويلُهما دقيقهما ممتدُّهما إلى مؤخر العين)
16. أَقْرَنُ (مقرُون الحاجبين، يتصل أحدهما بالآخر)
17. شَدِيدُ سَوَادِ الشَّعْرِ
18. إِذَا صَمَتَ عَلاهُ الْوَقَارُ (الرزانة والحِلْم)
19. وَإِذَا تَكَلَّمَ عَلاهُ الْبَهَاءُ (الحسن والجلال والعظمة)
20. أَجْمَلُ النَّاسِ وَأَبْهَاهُ مِنْ بَعِيدٍ وَأَحْسَنُهُ وَأَحْلاهُ مِنْ قَرِيبٍ.
21. حُلْوُ الْمَنْطِقِ فصل (بيِّن ظاهر، يفصل بين الحق والباطل)
22. لا نَزْرٌ ولا هَذْرٌ (ليس بقليل فيدل على عِيٍّ ولا كثير فاسد؛ لا قليل غير مفهوم ولا كثير مملّ)
23. كَأَنَّ مَنْطِقَهُ خَرَزَاتُ نَظْمٍ يَتَحَدَّرْنَ (كلامه محكم بليغ)
24. رَبْعَةٌ (مَرْبُوعُ الخَلْقِ لا بالطويل ولا بالقصير)
25. لا تَقْتَحِمُهُ عَيْنٌ مِنْ قِصَرٍ (لا تزدريه لقصره فتجاوزه الى غيره بل تهابه وتقبله وتعظمه) ولا تَشْنَؤُهُ مِنْ طُولٍ (لا يُبْغَضُ لفرط طوله)
26. غُصْنٌ بَيْنَ غُصْنَيْنِ فَهُوَ أَنْضَرُ الثلاثةِ مَنْظَرًا وَأَحْسَنُهُمْ قَدْرًا
27. لَهُ رُفَقَاءُ يَحُفُّونَ بِهِ. إِذَا قَالَ اسْتَمَعُوا لِقَوْلِهِ، وَإِذَا أَمَرَ تَبَادَرُوا إِلَى أَمْرِهِ
28. مَحْفُودٌ (مخدوم، يسرعون طاعة له) مَحْشُودٌ (الذي يجتمع الناس حوله ليمتثلوا قوله ويقتدوا بأفعاله)
29. لا عَابِسٌ (ليس الكريهَ المَلْقَى والجَهْمَ المُحيَّا)
30. وَلا مُفْنِدٌ (ليس لا فائدة في كلامه لكبرٍ أصابه أو لقلة عقله).

Masjid Quba

The Prophet ﷺ arrives in Quba.

The First Masjid in Islam

Referenced in the Quran:

لَا تَقُمۡ فِيۡهِ اَبَدًا ؕ لَمَسۡجِدٌ اُسِّسَ عَلَى التَّقۡوٰى مِنۡ اَوَّلِ يَوۡمٍ اَحَقُّ اَنۡ تَقُوۡمَ فِيۡهِ ؕ فِيۡهِ
رِجَالٌ يُّحِبُّوۡنَ اَنۡ يَّتَطَهَّرُوۡا ؕ وَ اللّٰهُ يُحِبُّ الۡمُطَّهِّرِيۡنَ ﴿۱۰۸﴾

Do not stand [for prayer] within it - ever. A mosque founded on righteousness from the first day is more worthy for you to stand in. Within it are men who love to purify themselves; and Allah loves those who purify themselves. [9:108]

On the 5th day, the Prophet W proceeded to Madinah, accompanied by Abu Bakr T

The First Jumu'ah

The first Jumu'ah in Islam took place between Quba and Madinah in the locality of Banu Salim.

Masjid Jumu'ah

Lessons from the First Khutbah:

Entry into Madinah

After the Jumu'ah, Prophet Muhammad ﷺ and Abu Bakr (RA) head to Madinah

Zubair and Talha (RA)

The Prophet's ﷺ Arrival in Madinah

Baraa ibn 'Aazib said: *"I have not witnessed the people of Madinah as ecstatic as they were on the day of The Prophet ﷺ arrived in Madinah".*

Rabbis and the Prophet ﷺ

ewish scholars were expecting the arrival of the Final Messenger ﷺ.

'assir ibn Akhtab

Abdullah ibn Salam

- Allah SWT describes this incident by saying:

قُلْ أَرَءَيْتُمْ إِن كَانَ مِنْ عِندِ اللَّهِ وَكَفَرْتُم بِهِ وَشَهِدَ شَاهِدٌ مِّنْ بَنِىٓ إِسْرَٰٓءِيلَ عَلَىٰ مِثْلِهِ
فَـَٔامَنَ وَاسْتَكْبَرْتُمْ ۖ إِنَّ اللَّهَ لَا يَهْدِى الْقَوْمَ الظَّٰلِمِينَ

Say, "Have you considered: if the Quran was form Allah and you disbelieved in it while a witness from the Children of Israel has testified to something similar and believed while you were arrogant?" Indeed, Allah does not guide the wrongdoing people. [46:10]

Rabbis and the Prophet ﷺ

The rabbis of Madinah assembled in Baitul-Mirdas upon the Prophet's ﷺ arrival.

The rabbis put forth a few questions for the Prophet ﷺ to answer.

The Prophet ﷺ recited Surah Yusuf which they found similar to the Torah.

The Prophet's ﷺ Seal of Prophethood

Islam of Maymun ibn Yaameen

House of Abu Ayyub (RA)

Upon arrival in Madinah, the Prophet's ﷺ camel settled in front of the home of Abu Ayyub (RA).

He was a descendant of the King of Tubba'.

Islam of Salman Al-Farisi (RA)

Salman Al-Farisi (RA) descended from the Persian emperors and was responsible for tending to the fire of the Zoroastrians.

- Converted Secretly to Christianity

- His Quest to Learn

- The Signs of Prophethood

- Salman Al-Farisi (RA) Accepts Islam

- The Prophet ﷺ helps Salman Al-Farisi (RA) buy his freedom

Brotherhood

:stablishing the Brotherhood Between the Muhajireen and Ansaar.

\ws and Khazraj became known as the Ansaar

- Ansaar: أَنصَارِ : the ones who provide support

- The Chief of Khazraj : Sa'd ibn 'Ubadah

- The Chief of Aws: Sa'd ibn Mu'ath

Anas (RA): *"None of the Ansaar would ever regard anyone more eligible to their wealth than their Muhaajir brother"*

Brotherhood

Brotherhood in Mecca

1. Abu Bakr رَضِوَٱللَّهُعَنْهُ & 'Umar رَضِوَٱللَّهُعَنْهُ
2. Hamzah رَضِوَٱللَّهُعَنْهُ & Zaid bin Haarisah رَضِوَٱللَّهُعَنْهُ
3. 'Usmaan Ghani رَضِوَٱللَّهُعَنْهُ & 'Abdur Rahmaan bin 'Awf رَضِوَٱللَّهُعَنْهُ
4. Zubair bin 'Awwaam رَضِوَٱللَّهُعَنْهُ & 'Abdullah bin Mas'ood رَضِوَٱللَّهُعَنْهُ
5. 'Ubaidah bin Haaris رَضِوَٱللَّهُعَنْهُ & Bilal bin Rabah رَضِوَٱللَّهُعَنْهُ
6. Mus'ab bin 'Umair رَضِوَٱللَّهُعَنْهُ & S'ad bin Abi Waqqaas رَضِوَٱللَّهُعَنْهُ
7. Abu 'Ubaidah رَضِوَٱللَّهُعَنْهُ & Saalim, slave of Huzaifah رَضِوَٱللَّهُعَنْهُ
8. Sa'eed bin Zaid رَضِوَٱللَّهُعَنْهُ & Talhah bin 'Ubaidullah رَضِوَٱللَّهُعَنْهُ
9. Sayyidina Rasulullah صَلَّىٱللَّهُعَلَيْهِوَسَلَّمَ & Ali رَضِوَٱللَّهُعَنْهُ

Brotherhood in Madinah

1. Abu Bakr Siddeeq رَضِوَٱللَّهُعَنْهُ & Khaarijah bin Zaid رَضِوَٱللَّهُعَنْهُ
2. 'Umar bin Khattaab رَضِوَٱللَّهُعَنْهُ & 'Atbaan bin Maalik رَضِوَٱللَّهُعَنْهُ
3. Abu 'Ubaidah bin Jarraah رَضِوَٱللَّهُعَنْهُ & S'ad bin Mu'aaz رَضِوَٱللَّهُعَنْهُ
4. 'Abdur-Rahmaan bin 'Awf رَضِوَٱللَّهُعَنْهُ & S'ad bin Rab'i رَضِوَٱللَّهُعَنْهُ
5. Zubair bin 'Awwaam رَضِوَٱللَّهُعَنْهُ & Salaamah bin Salaamah bin Wuqaish رَضِوَٱللَّهُعَنْهُ
6. 'Usmaan bin Affaan رَضِوَٱللَّهُعَنْهُ & Aws bin Saabit رَضِوَٱللَّهُعَنْهُ
7. Talhah bin 'Ubaidullah رَضِوَٱللَّهُعَنْهُ & K'ab bin Maalik رَضِوَٱللَّهُعَنْهُ
8. Sa'eed bin Zaid bin 'Amr bin Nufail رَضِوَٱللَّهُعَنْهُ & Ubayy bin K'ab رَضِوَٱللَّهُعَنْهُ
9. Mus'ab bin 'Umair رَضِوَٱللَّهُعَنْهُ & Abu Ayyub Khaalid bin Zaid Ansaari رَضِوَٱللَّهُعَنْهُ
10. Abu Huzaifah bin 'Utbah رَضِوَٱللَّهُعَنْهُ & 'Abbaad bin Bishr رَضِوَٱللَّهُعَنْهُ
11. 'Ammaar bin Yaasir رَضِوَٱللَّهُعَنْهُ & Huzaifah bin Yamaan رَضِوَٱللَّهُعَنْهُ

Brotherhood

السّٰبِقُوْنَ الْاَوَّلُوْنَ مِنَ الْمُهٰجِرِيْنَ وَ الْاَنْصَارِ وَ الَّذِيْنَ اتَّبَعُوْهُمْ بِاِحْسَانٍ ۙ رَّضِيَ اللّٰهُ عَنْهُمْ
وَ رَضُوْا عَنْهُ وَ اَعَدَّ لَهُمْ جَنّٰتٍ تَجْرِيْ تَحْتَهَا الْاَنْهٰرُ خٰلِدِيْنَ فِيْهَآ اَبَدًا ؕ ذٰلِكَ الْفَوْزُ الْعَظِيْمُ
﴿١٠٠﴾

And the first forerunners [in the faith] among the Muhajireen and the Ansar and those who followed them with good conduct – Allah is pleased with them and they are pleased with Him, and He has prepared for them gardens beneath which rivers flow, wherein they will abide forever. That is the great attainment. [9:100]

Modern Day Challenges

Acclimation to Madinah

Meccans were not accustomed to the weather of Madinah.

Many companions became sick and struggled to acclimate.

- Abu Bakr (RA)

- Bilal (RA)

Virtues of Madinah

When the Prophet ﷺ saw the companions struggling, he made a beautiful du'a for the city of Madinah:

عَنْ أَبِي هُرَيْرَةَرَضِىَ اللهُ عَنْهُ، أَنَّهُ قَالَ كَانَ النَّاسُ إِذَا رَأَوْا أَوَّلَ الثَّمَرِ جَاءُوا بِهِ إِلَى رَسُولِ اللهِ ﷺ فَإِذَا أَخَذَهُ رَسُولُ اللهِ ﷺ قَالَ " اللَّهُمَّ بَارِكْ لَنَا فِي ثَمَرِنَا وَبَارِكْ لَنَا فِي مَدِينَتِنَا وَبَارِكْ لَنَا فِي صَاعِنَا وَبَارِكْ لَنَا فِي مُدِّنَا اللَّهُمَّ إِنَّ إِبْرَاهِيمَ عَبْدُكَ وَخَلِيلُكَ وَنَبِيُّكَ وَإِنِّي عَبْدُكَ وَنَبِيُّكَ وَإِنَّهُ دَعَاكَ لِمَكَّةَ وَإِنِّي أَدْعُوكَ لِلْمَدِينَةِ بِمِثْلِ مَا دَعَاكَ بِهِ لِمَكَّةَ وَمِثْلِهِ مَعَهُ - ثُمَّ يَدْعُو أَصْغَرَ وَلِيدٍ يَرَاهُ فَيُعْطِيهِ ذَلِكَ الثَّمَرَ

When people saw the first fruits of the season, they brought them to the Messenger of Allah. The Messenger of Allah, took them and said, 'O Allah! Bless us in our fruits. Bless us in our city. Bless us in our harvest (Plentiful or little). O Allah! Ibrahim is Your slave, Your Khalil and Your Prophet. I am Your slave and Your Prophet. He prayed to You for Mecca. I pray to You for Madinah for the like of what he prayed to You for Mecca, and the like of it with it.' Then he called the smallest child he saw and gave him the fruits. [Muslim]

Construction of Masjid An-Nabawi

After arriving at the home of Abu Ayyub, one of the first initiatives taken by the Prophet ﷺ was establishing an area for a Masjid.

The land for the masjid was gifted by a man from Banu Najjar.

The Prophet ﷺ actively participated in construction of the masjid.

Ammar ibn Yassir

The Physical Structure of the Masjid

Virtues of Praying in Masjid An-Nabawi

Housing for the Prophet ﷺ and His Wives

urah Al-Hujurat was revealed about the etiquettes of the rooms of the Prophet ﷺ and his wives:

يٰٓاَيُّهَاالَّذِيْنَ اٰمَنُوْا لَا تَرْفَعُوْٓا اَصْوَاتَكُمْ فَوْقَ صَوْتِ النَّبِيِّ وَ لَا تَجْهَرُوْا لَهٗ بِالْقَوْلِ كَجَهْرِ
بَعْضِكُمْ لِبَعْضٍ اَنْ تَحْبَطَ اَعْمَالُكُمْ وَ اَنْتُمْ لَا تَشْعُرُوْنَ ﴿٢﴾ اِنَّ الَّذِيْنَ يَغُضُّوْنَ
اَصْوَاتَهُمْ عِنْدَ رَسُوْلِ اللّٰهِ اُولٰٓئِكَ الَّذِيْنَ امْتَحَنَ اللّٰهُ قُلُوْبَهُمْ لِلتَّقْوٰى ۭ لَهُمْ مَّغْفِرَةٌ وَّ
اَجْرٌ عَظِيْمٌ ﴿٣﴾ اِنَّ الَّذِيْنَ يُنَادُوْنَكَ مِنْ وَّرَآءِ الْحُجُرٰتِ اَكْثَرُهُمْ لَا يَعْقِلُوْنَ ﴿٤﴾ وَ
لَوْ اَنَّهُمْ صَبَرُوْا حَتّٰى تَخْرُجَ اِلَيْهِمْ لَكَانَ خَيْرًا لَّهُمْ ۭ وَ اللّٰهُ غَفُوْرٌ رَّحِيْمٌ ﴿٥﴾

O ye who believe! Raise not your voices above the voice of the Prophet, nor speak aloud to him in talk, as ye may speak aloud to one another, lest your deeds become vain and ye perceive not (2) Those that lower their voices in the presence of Allah's Messenger,- their hearts has Allah tested for piety: for them is Forgiveness and a great Reward (3) Those who shout out to thee from without the inner apartments - most of them lack understanding (4) If only they had patience until thou come out to them, it would be best for them: And Allah is Most-Forgiving, Most Merciful (5) [49:2-5]

All of the structures were extremely simple show the humility of the Prophet ﷺ .

Abu Umaamah: *"If only the original structure of the rooms were left intact, people would have witnessed for themselves how the messenger ﷺ who was divinely awarded the keys to the treasures of the world passed his life in such simple rooms and huts."*

Ashaab al-Suffa

These were companions who lived in Madinah and were extremely poor.

Suffa: Ledge

These companions were extremely dedicated to knowledge.

- Abu Hurayrah (RA)

Impact of Ashaab al-Suffah in our lives

Treaty with the Jewish Tribes

Majority of the population of Madinah was made up of 2 tribes: Aws & Khazraj

A large number of Jews lived on the outskirts of Madinah. There were 3 major tribes:

- Banu Qaynuqa'
- Banu Nadheer
- Banu Quraydha

The Prophet W had a treaty written with the Jews of Madinah to ensure loyalty and security.

"In the name of Allah, the Compassionate, the Merciful. This is a document from Muhammad, the Prophet, governing the relation between the Believers from among the Muhajirun and Ansar and those who followed them, joined them, and strived with them. They form one and the same community as against the rest of men."

"The Jews shall maintain their own religion and the Muslims theirs. Loyalty is a protection against treachery. The close friends of Jews are as themselves. None of them shall go out on a military expedition except with the permission of Muhammad, but he shall not be prevented from taking revenge for a wound.

"The Jews shall be responsible for their expenses and the Believers for theirs. Each, if attacked, shall come to the assistance of the other."

"Allah approves the truth and goodwill of this covenant. This treaty shall not protect the unjust or the criminal. Whoever goes out to fight as well as whoever stays at home shall be safe and secure in this city unless he has perpetrated an injustice or committed a crime.... Allah is the protector of the good and God-fearing people."

Inception of Adhan

The Prophet ﷺ and the companions discussed how prayer should be announced.

اللهُ أَكْبَرُ اللهُ أَكْبَرُ

اللهُ أَكْبَرُ اللهُ أَكْبَرُ

Ideas for the Call to Prayer

أَشْهَدُ أَنْ لَا إِلٰهَ إِلَّا اللهُ أَشْهَدُ أَنْ لَا إِلٰهَ إِلَّا اللهُ

وَأَشْهَدُ أَنَّ مُحَمَّدًا رَسُولُ اللهِ وَأَشْهَدُ أَنَّ مُحَمَّدًا رَسُولُ اللهِ

Dream of Abdullah ibn Zayd (RA) & Umar ibn Al-Khattab (RA)

حَيَّ عَلَى الصَّلَاةِ حَيَّ عَلَى الصَّلَاةِ

حَيَّ عَلَى الْفَلَاحِ حَيَّ عَلَى الْفَلَاحِ

اللهُ أَكْبَرُ اللهُ أَكْبَرُ

لَا إِلٰهَ إِلَّا اللهُ

Bilal: The Mua'dhin

اللَّهُمَّ رَبَّ هَذِهِ الدَّعْوَةِ التَّامَّةِ، وَالصَّلَاةِ الْقَائِمَةِ، آتِ سَيِّدَنا مُحَمَّداً
الْوَسِيلَةَ وَالْفَضِيلَةَ، [والدَّرَجَةَ الرَّفِيعَة] وَابْعَثْهُ مَقاماً مَحْمُوداً الَّذِي
وَعَدْتَهُ، [إِنَّكَ لَا تُخْلِفُ الْمِيعَادَ]

O Allah, Lord of this most perfect call, and of the Prayer that is about to be established, grant to our Master Muhammad the intercession and favor [and the highest rank], and exalt him to a position of glory that You have promised him. [Verily You do not neglect promises].

The Significance of the Adhan

The Water of Madinah

When the Muslims first arrived there was a water shortage.

Meccans were accustomed to drinking ZamZam.

Well of Ruma

The Companion who Purchased Jannah Twice

Marriage with 'Aisha (RA)

'Aisha's (RA) marriage to the Prophet ﷺ

Difference of Opinion on the Age of 'Aisha (RA)

Virtues of 'Aisha (RA)

'he Knowledge of 'Aisha (RA)

- Transmitted Over 2000 Ahadith
    - Only seven companions transmitted more than 1000 narrations.
- Some scholars have even said: *"One fourth of Islamic knowledge has reached us through 'Aisha".*

Defense of 'Aisha (RA) in the Quran (10 verses)

Most Beloved to the Prophet ﷺ

Change of Qiblah

The initial Qiblah faced toward Jerusalem.

In Mecca, the Prophet ﷺ would face Jerusalem, while also facing the Ka'bah.

The Changing of the Qiblah:

- 15th of Sha'ban, 2 A.H. 16 months after Hijrah
- Dhuhr Prayer in Masjid Qiblatain

Response from the Jews of Madinah

Ramadan, Eid, and Zakat are Legislated

amadan was instituted in Sha'ban

:id Al-Fitr came at the end of Ramadan along with Zakat Al-Fitr

Eid Al-Adha also became mandatory in this year despite the fact there was no Hajj.

Military Expeditions

What is Jihad?

Jahada: جهد Literally means to struggle

- Internal and external struggle
- The ideology of Islam

There are two types of military expeditions during the life of the Prophet ﷺ

- Sariyya سرية
- Ghazwa غزوة

Throughout Madinah there were 38 Sarriya and 21 Ghazwa.

The first Sarriya ever sent was led by Hamza (RA) and was made up of 30 muhajireen.

- They went to Saif al-Bahr to scout a trade caravan of 300 led by Abu Jahl
- No battle took place

Military Expeditions

'he next Sarriya was sent a month later in Shawwal led by 'Ubaida ibn Harith

- Consisted of 60-80 muhajireen, also went to scout a caravan
- One arrow was fired by Sa'd ibn Abi Waqqas (RA)
    - First arrow fired in Islam
- No battle took place

ꞩa'd ibn Abi Waqqas (RA) led a Sarriya in Dhul Qa'dah in the first year of Hijrah

- 20 muhajireen went in pursuit of a caravan
- They would hide in the daytime and only travel at night
- No battle took place

The expeditions were made up of mostly Muhajireen.

- Where are the Ansar?

The first Ghazwa to take place was the Ghazwa to Abwa

- The Prophet ﷺ placed Sa'd ibn 'Ubadah (RA) in charge of Madinah
- In the month of Safar, 60 Muhajireen accompanied the Prophet ﷺ in pursuit of a caravan
- No battle took place
- Truce formed with tribe of Banu Damra

Military Expeditions

The Ghazwa of Bawaat took place in Rabi' Al-Awwal/Al-Thaani in the second year of Hijrah

- Sa'd ibn Mu'ath (RA) was put in charge of Madinah
- 200 muhajireen set out in pursuit of a large caravan
- The caravan slipped away and they returned back to Madinah without a battle taking place

Important Note

- Only eight out of the 21 Ghazwat that took place involved physical combat
- Badr, Uhud, Ahzab (aka Khandaq), Muraysiya, Banu Quraidha, Khaybar, Mecca (Fath Mecca), and Hunayn

Expedition of Ushayrah (Jumaadal-Ula, 2 A.H.)

- Abu Salamah ibn 'Abdul-Asad (RA) in charge of Madinah.
- The Prophet ﷺ set out with 200 muhajireen and 30 camels in pursuit of a caravan
- The Prophet ﷺ formed a peace treaty with the tribe of Bani Mudlij
- No battle took place

Minor Battle at Badr

- Ten days after the Muslims returned to Madinah, an attack was launched at night
- Kurz ibn Jabir Al-Fahri made off with a number of Muslim's camels and goats
    - Kurz ibn Jabir was a chief of Quraysh, he later embraced Islam
- The Prophet ﷺ immediately set out in pursuit, until reaching an area near Badr

Military Expeditions

'he next Sarriya that was sent was led by Abdullah ibn Jahsh (RA)

11 muhajireen dispatched with him in the month of Rajab

They were sent out to gather intelligence about the Quraysh and their movements

While doing this, they attacked a passing Qurayshi caravan, killing one person and seizing their goods

- This took place in the month of Rajab, a month in which fighting is prohibited
- The companions thought the first day Sha'ban had begun when they attacked, but it was actually the last day of Rajab

The Prophet ﷺ did not allow anyone to take spoils of war until Allah SWT revealed a ruling through this ayah:

يَسْأَلُونَكَ عَنِ الشَّهْرِ الْحَرَامِ قِتَالٍ فِيهِ ۖ قُلْ قِتَالٌ فِيهِ كَبِيرٌ ۖ وَصَدٌّ عَن سَبِيلِ اللَّهِ وَكُفْرٌ بِهِ وَالْمَسْجِدِ الْحَرَامِ وَإِخْرَاجُ أَهْلِهِ مِنْهُ أَكْبَرُ عِندَ اللَّهِ ۚ وَالْفِتْنَةُ أَكْبَرُ مِنَ الْقَتْلِ ۗ وَلَا يَزَالُونَ يُقَاتِلُونَكُمْ حَتَّىٰ يَرُدُّوكُمْ عَن دِينِكُمْ إِنِ اسْتَطَاعُوا ۚ وَمَن يَرْتَدِدْ مِنكُمْ عَن دِينِهِ فَيَمُتْ وَهُوَ كَافِرٌ فَأُولَٰئِكَ حَبِطَتْ أَعْمَالُهُمْ فِي الدُّنْيَا وَالْآخِرَةِ ۖ وَأُولَٰئِكَ أَصْحَابُ النَّارِ ۖ هُمْ فِيهَا خَالِدُونَ

They ask you about the sacred month - about fighting therein. Say, "Fighting therein is great [sin], but averting [people] from the way of Allah and disbelief in Him and [preventing access to] al-Masjid al-Haram and the expulsion of its people therefrom are greater [evil] in the sight of Allah. And fitnah is greater than killing." And they will continue to fight you until they turn you back from your religion if they are able. And whoever of you reverts from his religion [to disbelief] and dies while he is a disbeliever - for those, their deeds have become worthless in this world and the Hereafter, and those are the companions of the Fire, they will abide therein eternally [2:217}

Events that Led to Badr

The Prophet ﷺ learned that Abu Sufyan was returning to Mecca with a trade caravan transporting commercial merchandise and goods from Syria.

- The Prophet ﷺ had gathered the companions to proceed towards the caravan
    - They did not expect there to be a battle
    - The Muslims prepared very quickly and did not have time to gather many resources

- On the 12th of Ramadan, a total of 313 Muslims left Madinah with only two horses and 70 camels

- A mile out of Madinah, the army was inspected for youngsters
    - A few youngsters were sent back to Madinah because they were too young to join the battle
- There were three battle flags carried by Muslims
    - Ali (RA)
    - Mus'ab ibn Umair (RA), Carrying the main flag
    - Sa'd ibn Mu'ath (RA)

Retaliation of Abu Sufyan

- Upon hearing news of the Muslims, Abu Sufyan sent a messenger to Mecca to inform them and call for troops
- The Meccans gathered an army of 1000 troops led by Abu Jahl
    - Included 100 horsemen and 600 men in full armor
    - All tribes participated in this except for the tribe of Umar (RA): Banu 'Adi

Events that Led to Badr

Jpon hearing of the army of the Meccans, the Prophet ﷺ consulted the companions

- The Muhajireen immediately began expressing their allegiance and willingness to proceed
- Miqdaad ibn Al-Aswad and Sa'd ibn Mu'ath (RA) gave powerful speeches showing their allegiance to the Prophet ﷺ

Dream of 'Atikah bint Abdul Muttalib

When the Quraysh gathered on the battlefield, 'Utbah ibn Rabi'ah addressed them in a speech

- He tried to show them that there is no benefit in fighting, as these were their relatives and tribe members
- He proposed that that Quraysh leave their fate to the rest of the Arabs who can finish off the Muslims
- Abu Jahl heard this speech and dismissed him as cowardly

The Prophet ﷺ also consulted the companions regarding where they should set up camp

- Hubaab ibn Munthir (RA) advised the Prophet ﷺ

Before the Battle

The day before Badr, the Prophet ﷺ took his companions out to the battlefield and marked the locations were certain people would fall.

Anas (RA) says:

> *"By Allah SWT none of them fell more than a hairs length from the area he described."*

Du'a of the Prophet ﷺ the night before Badr

Ali (RA) narrates:

> *"On the night preceding the battle of Badr, there was not a single one of us who did not fall off to sleep except the messenger of Allah SWT. He spent the entire night in prayer and du'a until the morning."*

While straightening the lines of the soldiers a companion named Sawaad ibn Ghaziyyah was out of line

- The Prophet ﷺ nudged him into line and he complained that he was pushed harder than the others

- The Justice of the Prophet ﷺ

Before the Battle

Mubaarazah: Three vs. Three

- This is a stage before the battle in which three members of each army go out and fight in a small battle
- Initially, the Muslims sent three Ansari companions and the Quraysh rejected them

Ali (RA) vs. Waleed ibn 'Utbah

Hamzah (RA) vs. Shaybah ibn Rabi'ah

'Ubaidah ibn Al-Harith (RA) vs. 'Utbah ibn Rabi'ah

- Ali (RA) and Hamza (RA) quickly defeated their opponents while 'Ubaidah (RA) was severely injured

Abu Jahl made du'a before the battle ensued:

"O Allah! He who is guilty amongst us of severing family ties and of perpetrating strange actions, O Allah destroy him, and amongst us, he who is most dear and beloved to You, O Allah, grant him victory."

Allah SWT responded to this with the following Verse:

إِنْ تَسْتَفْتِحُوا فَقَدْ جَاءَكُمُ الْفَتْحُ ۖ وَإِنْ تَنْتَهُوا فَهُوَ خَيْرٌ لَكُمْ ۖ وَإِنْ تَعُودُوا نَعُدْ ۖ وَلَنْ تُغْنِيَ
عَنْكُمْ فِئَتُكُمْ شَيْئًا وَلَوْ كَثُرَتْ ۙ وَأَنَّ اللَّهَ مَعَ الْمُؤْمِنِينَ ﴿١٩﴾

(O disbelievers!) You were seeking victory. So, here victory has come unto you. And if you desist (from evil) it will be better for you. And if you return (to fight) so shall We return and your forces will be of no avail to you however numerous they may be Verily Allah is with the believers. [8:19]

Battle of Badr

Du'a of the Prophet ﷺ during the battle of Badr

This group of Muslims was the only chance Islam had to survive; if they were defeated the religion would have been in jeopardy.

Descent of the Angels to Assist the Muslims

- Jibreel, Mikaeel, and Israfeel were commanding the Angels in battle
- Allah SWT sent down 1000, then 3000, and finally 5000 angels in support of the Muslims

اِذْ تَقُوْلُ لِلْمُؤْمِنِيْنَ اَلَنْ يَّكْفِيَكُمْ اَنْ يُّمِدَّكُمْ رَبُّكُمْ بِثَلٰثَةِ اٰلٰفٍ مِّنَ الْمَلٰٓئِكَةِ مُنْزَلِيْنَ ﴿١٢٤﴾
بَلٰى ۚ اِنْ تَصْبِرُوْا وَ تَتَّقُوْا وَ يَاْتُوْكُمْ مِّنْ فَوْرِهِمْ هٰذَا يُمْدِدْكُمْ رَبُّكُمْ بِخَمْسَةِ اٰلٰفٍ مِّنَ الْمَلٰٓئِكَةِ
مُسَوِّمِيْنَ ﴿١٢٥﴾

[Remember] when you said to the believers, "is it not sufficient for you that your Lord should reinforce you with three thousand angels sent down? (124) Yes, if you remain patient and conscious of Allah SWT and the enemy come upon you [attacking] in rage, your Lord will reinforce you with five thousand angels having marks [of distinction]" (125) [3:124-125]

The Battle of Badr

Abu Usaid As-Sa'idi (who attended the Battle of Badr) related: *"On the day of the battle of Badr, the angels descended from the skies wearing yellow turbans. The tail ends of their turbans were suspended between their shoulders. Zubair was himself wearing a yellow turban on the day of this battle."*

The companions were overcome with a feeling of security and tranquility

- They were outnumbered 3:1 yet with the aid of the angels they would outnumber the Meccans 5:1

At this point, the Muslims defeated the Meccans with ease

- Many of the chieftains of Mecca were killed in this battle
    - Abu Jahl was killed by two young boys from Madinah
        - They had never seen Abu Jahl, so Abdul Rahman ibn 'Awf (RA) identified him, and the young boys then targeted him in the battle
    - Umayyah ibn Khalaf was killed despite Abdul Rahman ibn 'Awf (RA) trying to protect him and take him as a prisoner.
        - Ummayah ibn Khalaf tortured Bilal (RA) in Mecca
        - Bilal (RA) called out to the Ansar about his presence on the battlefield and he was killed.

Aftermath of the Battle of Badr

News Of Victory

- The Prophet ﷺ dispatched his messengers to Madinah to inform them of the victory
    - 'Abdullah ibn Rawaahah (RA) towards the upper regions
    - Zaid ibn Harithah (RA) towards the lower regions of Madinah

A total of 70 Meccans were killed ,70 were taken as prisoners, and 14 Companions were martyred.

The Muslims had to fight their own family members, who were still disbelievers, in this battle

- Abu Ubaydah (RA) fought his father

- Abbas (RA) fought against the Muslims

- Abu Bakr (RA) fought against his son

- Mus'ab ibn Umair (RA) fought against his brother

Aftermath of the Battle of Badr

Prisoners of War

- There was a dispute on what should be done with the prisoners of war
- 'Umar (RA) said they should be killed, but the Prophet ﷺ sided with Abu Bakr (RA) in ransoming them
- 'Umar (RA) was concerned that, if released, they would return fight the Muslims later (This happened in Battle of Uhud)

Allah SWT revealed verses of the Quran stating that they should not have been ransomed

مَا كَانَ لِنَبِيٍّ اَنْ يَّكُوْنَ لَهٗٓ اَسْرٰى حَتّٰى يُثْخِنَ فِي الْاَرْضِ ۭ تُرِيْدُوْنَ عَرَضَ الدُّنْيَا ڰ وَاللّٰهُ يُرِيْدُ الْاٰخِرَةَ ۭ وَاللّٰهُ عَزِيْزٌ حَكِيْمٌ ﴿٦٧﴾

It is not for a prophet to have captives [of war] until he inflicts a massacre [upon Allah's enemies] in the land. Some Muslims desire the commodities of this world, but Allah desires [for you] the Hereafter. And Allah is Exalted in Might and Wise. [8:67]

Among those ransomed was Abu Al-'Aas, the husband of Zaynab (RA), the Prophet's ﷺ daughter

- She sent Khadijah's (RA) necklace as a ransom for her husband.
- The Prophet ﷺ became emotional upon seeing this and freed her husband on the condition he sends her to Madinah.
- They could no longer live together because she was Muslim and he was a Polytheist.

Aftermath of the Battle of Badr

Zaynab's (RA) Migration

Abu Al-'Aas accepted Islam in the seventh year after Hijrah.

Other Prisoners of War

- Abu Aziz, the brother of Mus'ab ibn Umair (RA)

- Abbas, the uncle of the Prophet ﷺ

Aftermath of the Battle of Badr

Hatim ibn Abi Balta'a (RA) was a companion at Badr

- He was scared for his family at the conquest of Mecca, so he attempted to inform the Meccans of the conquest
- The Prophet ﷺ was told about this and he was pardoned due to his sincerity and his status as a Companion at Badr.

The Prophet ﷺ said about them:

عَنْ أَبِي هُرَيْرَةَ رَضِيَ اللهُ عَنْهُ أَنَّ النَّبِيَّ ﷺ قال:"إِنَّ اللهَ اطَّلَعَ عَلَى أَهْلِ بَدْرٍ فَقَالَ اعْمَلُوا مَا شِئْتُمْ فَقَدْ غَفَرْتُ لَكُمْ"

Allah SWT has looked upon the people of Badr and said: "Do what you wish Allah SWT has forgiven you"

[Bukhari]

Virtues of the People of Badr

Aftermath of the Battle of Badr

Reaction of the Meccans after Defeat

- They invested the loot of the Badr caravan into preparations for Uhud

- The first person from Quraysh to enter Mecca announced:

"'Utbah ibn Rabi'ah has been killed, Shaybah ibn Rabi'ah has been killed, Abul-Hakam ibn Hishaam (Abu Jahal) has been killed, Umayyah ibn Khalaf has been killed, Zam'ah ibn Aswad has been killed, Nabihah ibn Hajaaj has been killed, Munabbihah ibn Hajaaj has been killed, so and so has been killed."

Death of Abu Lahab

Madinah After the Battle of Badr

assing of Ruqayyah bint Muhammad (RA) and the Grief of 'Uthman (RA)

Marriage of Ali (RA) and Fatima (RA)

The Prophet ﷺ prayed the first ever Eid prayer with the companions.

Umair ibn Wahab (RA) Accepts Islam

Madinah After the Battle of Badr

After the Muslims victory at Badr, the Jews of Banu Qaynuqa' began to show animosity towards the Muslims despite their treaty.

- They violated the treaty
- Muslims advanced towards them with an army
- They barricaded themselves in a fortress for 15 days until the beginning of Dhul Qa'da
- They surrendered out of fear and the Prophet ﷺ expelled them from the region

Assassination of Ka'ab ibn al-ashraf

- Ka'ab ibn Al-Ashraf was a poet who composed poems insulting the Prophet ﷺ
- Importance of poetry amongst the early Arabs
- He traveled to Mecca after Badr and encouraged Quraysh to avenge their defeat of Badr
- Muhammad ibn Maslamah, 'Abbad ibn Bishr, and Abu Na'ilah (RA) went out to assassinate him

Uthman ibn Madh'oon Passes Away

Events Leading to Uhud

he Battle of Uhud took place after the Muslims were victorious at Badr

Meccans were seeking revenge and were enraged at their loss

They formed an army of 3000, rallying many tribes from the region

Varning of Abbas (RA) to the Prophet ﷺ

- Abbas collected information about the Meccan plot
- He sent his fastest messenger to ensure the Prophet ﷺ would receive the message within three days
- The Prophet ﷺ dispatched two companions to investigate

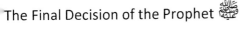

Habbaab ibn Munthir (RA) scouted the size of the Meccan army

Consultation with the Companions

The Final Decision of the Prophet 

- The Prophet ﷺ eventually sided with the youth of Madinah
- The Prophet ﷺ emerged with his armor on and the younger companions felt guilty for compelling him to change his decision

He Said: *"It is not permissible for a prophet to arm himself in preparation for war and subsequently remove his armor without engaging the enemy of Allah SWT in war".*

Prophet Muhammad ﷺ Departs from Madinah

- On the 11th of Shawwal, 3 A.H., the Prophet ﷺ departs from Madinah with 1000 Muslims: 100 fully armed and 2 horses

Abdullah ibn Ubayy and 300 Hypocrites Abandon the Army

Commencement of the Battle & the Initial Victory of the Muslims

Abu Dujanah

The Fate of Ubayy ibn Khalaf

- The Prophet ﷺ lightly scratched Ubayy with his spear during the Battle of Uhud
- He passed away on the way back to Mecca

The 50 Archers at the Battle of Uhud

Death of Hamzah T and Mus'ab T

Hamzah's (RA) Role in the battle

- Fought viciously in battle
- Hamzah (RA) was killed by Wahshee, the slave of Jubair ibn Mut'im

Hamzah's (RA) Mutilation

Death of Mus'ab (RA)

- Mus'ab ibn 'Umair (RA) was standing close to the Prophet ﷺ
- He defended the Prophet ﷺ valiantly until he was martyred
- Thereafter, the Prophet ﷺ gave the flag to Ali (RA)

Companions in Uhud

There were 14 companions who did not leave the side of the Prophet ﷺ during the Battle of Uhud

- Seven Ansar and seven Muhajireen
    - Talha ibn Ubaidillah (RA)
    - Sa'd ibn Abi Waqqas (RA)
    - Abu 'Ubaidah ibn Al-Jarrah (RA)

Utbah ibn Abi Waqqas and the Injuries of the Prophet ﷺ

The rumors of Prophet Muhammad's ﷺ death had spread, and the Quraysh started celebrating.

Mutilation of the Muslim Martyrs

- 'Amr Ibn Jamuh (RA)
- Mus'ab ibn Umair (RA)
- Hamzah ibn Abd al-Muttalib (RA)
- Abdullah ibn Jahsh (RA)
- Handhalah (RA)

Companions in Uhud

ther notable companions:

- Hamnah bint Jahsh (RA)

- Nusaybah (RA)

- Qatadah ibn Nouman (RA)

- Jabir (RA)

Aftermath of the Battle of Uhud

Abu Sufyan

The Prophet ﷺ Prays upon the Martyrs

The Prophet ﷺ Reacts to Hamzah's (RA) Death

Allah SWT revealed the following verse pardoning the archers and Muslims who fled out of panic:

إِنَّ الَّذِيْنَ تَوَلَّوْا مِنْكُمْ يَوْمَ الْتَقَى الْجَمْعٰنِ ۙ اِنَّمَا اسْتَزَلَّهُمُ الشَّيْطٰنُ بِبَعْضِ مَا كَسَبُوْا ۚ وَ لَقَدْ
عَفَا اللّٰهُ عَنْهُمْ ۗ اِنَّ اللّٰهَ غَفُوْرٌ حَلِيْمٌ ﴿١٥٥﴾ ٪

Translation: Indeed, those of you who turned back on the day the two armies met, it was Satan who caused them to slip because of some [blame] they had earned. But Allah SWT has already forgiven them. Indeed, Allah SWT is Forgiving and Forbearing. [3:155]

Lessons from the Battle of Uhud

essons:

Disobeying the Prophet ﷺ

- This battle shows that even in the most extreme situations, Allah SWT will not give victory to those who disobey the Prophet ﷺ

- In our times we can see the negative effects of leaving the prophetic traditions

- Allah SWT showed the companions difficulty in order to teach them that the Prophet ﷺ is the highest priority in any situation

Du'a For Istikhara:

اللَّهُمَّ إِنِّي أَسْتَخِيرُكَ بِعِلْمَكَ، وَأَسْتَقْدِرُكَ بِقُدْرَتِكَ، وَأَسأَلُكَ مِنْ فَضْلِكَ الْعَظِيمِ، فَإِنَّكَ تَقْدِرُ وَلَا أَقْدِرُ، وَتَعْلَمُ، وَلَا أَعْلَمُ، وَأَنْتَ عَلَّامُ الْغُيُوبِ، اللَّهُمَّ إِنْ كُنْتَ تَعْلَمُ أَنَّ هَذَا الأَمْرَ خَيْرٌ لِي فِي دِينِي وَمَعَاشِي وَعَاقِبَةِ أَمْرِي عَاجِلِهِ وَآجِلِهِ فَاقْدُرْهُ لِي وَيَسِّرْهُ لِي ثُمَّ بَارِكْ لِي فِيهِ، وَإِنْ كُنْتَ تَعْلَمُ أَنَّ هَذَا الأَمْرَ شَرٌّ لِي فِي دِينِي وَمَعَاشِي وَعَاقِبَةِ أَمْرِي عَاجِلِهِ وَآجِلِهِ فَاصْرِفْهُ عَنِّي وَاصْرِفْنِي عَنْهُ وَاقْدُرْ لِيَ الْخَيْرَ حَيْثُ كَانَ ثُمَّ أَرْضِنِي بِهِ

O Allah, I seek the counsel of Your Knowledge, and I seek the help of Your Omnipotence, and I beseech You for Your Magnificent Grace. Surely, You are Capable and I am not. You know and I know not, and You are the Knower of the unseen. O Allah, if You know that this matter [then mention the thing to be decided] is good for me in my religion and in my life and for my welfare in the life to come, - [or say: in this life and the afterlife] - then ordain it for me and make it easy for me, then bless me in it. And if You know that this matter is bad for me in my religion and in my life and for my welfare in the life to come, - [or say: in this life and the afterlife] - then distance it from me, and distance me from it, and ordain for me what is good wherever it may be, and help me to be content with it. [Bukhari]

Events of 3 A.H.

56

Marriage of the Prophet ﷺ and Hafsah (RA)

'Umar (RA) proposes Hafsah (RA) to Abu Bakr (RA) and 'Uthman (RA)

The Birth of Hasan (RA)

Alcohol was gradually prohibited

يَسْئَلُوْنَكَ عَنِ الْخَمْرِ وَ الْمَيْسِرِ قُلْ فِيْهِمَآ اِثْمٌ كَبِيْرٌ وَّ مَنَافِعُ لِلنَّاسِ وَ اِثْمُهُمَآ اَكْبَرُ مِنْ
نَّفْعِهِمَا وَ يَسْئَلُوْنَكَ مَا ذَا يُنْفِقُوْنَ قُلِ الْعَفْوَ كَذٰلِكَ يُبَيِّنُ اللّٰهُ لَكُمُ الْاٰيٰتِ لَعَلَّكُمْ
تَتَفَكَّرُوْنَ ﴿٢١٩﴾

They as you about wine and gambling. Say, In both there is great sin, and some benefits for people. And their sin is greater than their benefit. And they ask you as to what they should spend. Say, the surplus. This is how Allah makes His verses clear to you, so that you may ponder [2:219]

3

Incident of Raji'

During the month of Safar, some members of the 'Adal and Qura' tribes appeared before the Prophet ﷺ

- Of ten Companions sent, seven were martyred and three were captured
    - Among the three, 'Asim ibn Thabit (RA) was killed immediately and the other two were killed in Mecca after being sold as slaves.

Bi'r Ma'unah

he Prophet ﷺ was requested to send some companions to teach Islam near the region of Najd

The Prophet ﷺ was concerned but he sent 70 ansar, referred to as Al-Qurra', or "The Reciters of the Quran"

Well of Ma'unah

- All of them were killed except for Ka'b ibn Zaid (RA)
- The news of this incident and the news of Raji' reached him at the same time
- The Prophet (RA) was extremely grieved and supplicated against the transgressors

This prayer is referred to as Qunoot Al-Nazilah or "The prayer of the calamity"

اَللّٰهُمَّ اهْدِنِىْ فِيْمَنْ هَدَيْتَ وَ عَافِنِىْ فِيْمَنْ عَافَيْتَ وَ تَوَلَّنِىْ فِيْمَنْ تَوَلَّيْتَ وَ بَارِكْ لِىْ فِىْ مَآ اَعْطَيْتَ وَقِنِى شَرَّ مَا قَضَيْتَ فَاِنَّكَ تَقْضِىْ وَلَا يُقْضٰى عَلَيْكَ اِنَّهُ لَا يَذِلُّ مَنْ وَّالَيْتَ وَلَا يَعِزُّ مَنْ عَادَيْتَ تَبَارَكْتَ رَبَّنَا وَ تَعَالَيْتَ

O Allah! grant me guidance (and make me from) among those You have guided Grant me Well-being among those You have granted well-being Count me from among your allies and bless me in all You have granted me Protect me from (any) evil (resulting out) of your Decree Verily judgment is Your prerogative and none can overturn Your judgment Certainly! No disgrace can touch he whom You have befriended nor honor he who incites Your enmity. [Ibn Hibban]

Battle of Banu Nadheer

Causes for Battle:

- 'Amr ibn Ummayah Al-Dhamri killed two men from Banu 'Aamir
- He did this in revenge for the incident of Bi'r Ma'unah
- He was not aware that the Prophet ﷺ made a treaty with them
- Banu 'Aamir was allied with Banu Nadheer

Blood Money

Secret Assassination Plot

The Muslims besieged Banu Nadheer

Prohibition of Liquor

Alcohol was a key part of Arab society before Islam

Umar ibn Al-Khattab (RA) Makes Du'a

A companion was praying while intoxicated

يَٰٓأَيُّهَا ٱلَّذِينَ ءَامَنُوٓا إِنَّمَا ٱلْخَمْرُ وَ ٱلْمَيْسِرُ وَ ٱلْأَنصَابُ وَ ٱلْأَزْلَٰمُ رِجْسٌ مِّنْ عَمَلِ ٱلشَّيْطَٰنِ
فَٱجْتَنِبُوهُ لَعَلَّكُمْ تُفْلِحُونَ ﴿٩٠﴾

O you who believe! Wine, gambling, altars and divining arrows are filth, made up by Satan. Therefore, refrain from it, so that you may be successful [5:90]

The Expedition of Dhaat ur Riqaa'

This expedition took place in 4 A.H., in Rabi' ul-Akhir.

Information reached the Prophet ﷺ that Banu Mahaarib and Banu Tha'labah were preparing for war against the Muslims.

Salatul-Khawf

This expedition was referred to as Dhaatur-Riqaa'

- Riqaa' means rags or patches.
- Due to the harsh terrain, the companions had to wrap rags around their feet to prevent them from harm
- Dhaatur-Riqaa' is also the name of a mountain where the Prophet W camped during this expedition

The Expedition of Banu Mustaliq

ause of the Expedition of Banu Mustaliq

- Received news that the leader of the Banu Mustaliq tribe, Harith ibn Abi Diraar, had gathered a huge force and was preparing to launch an attack against the Muslims.
- Muslims set out with 700 men and 30 horses

Muslims defeat Banu Mustaliq

- The Muslims seized 2,000 camels and 5,000 thousand goats.
- Two hundred families were captured as prisoners.

The Prophet's ﷺ marriage to Juwayriya (RA)

The ruling of tayammum was revealed on the way back from Banu Mustaliq:

وَإِنْ كُنْتُمْ مَّرْضٰٓى اَوْ عَلٰى سَفَرٍ اَوْ جَآءَ اَحَدٌ مِّنْكُمْ مِّنَ الْغَآئِطِ اَوْ لٰمَسْتُمُ النِّسَآءَ فَلَمْ
تَجِدُوْا مَآءً فَتَيَمَّمُوْا صَعِيْدًا طَيِّبًا فَامْسَحُوْا بِوُجُوْهِكُمْ وَ اَيْدِيْكُمْ ۗ اِنَّ اللّٰهَ كَانَ عَفُوًّا غَفُوْرًا
﴿٤٣﴾

If you are either ill or traveling or have satisfied a want of nature or have had contact with women and can find no water, then betake yourselves to pure earth, passing with it lightly over your face and your hands. Surely Allah is All-Relenting, All-Forgiving. [4:43]

5

Incident of Slander

On the return from Banu Mustaliq, 'Aisha (RA) was separated from the caravan.

Safwaan ibn Mu'attal Al-Sulami

'Aisha (RA) returns to Madinah and falls sick

Rumors Start Spreading

Umm Mista'

The Cry of the Mother of the Believers (RA)

The Prophet ﷺ asks Bareera, the servant of 'Aisha (RA) about the rumors.

The main companions involved in this gossip:

- Mista' ibn Uthaathah (RA)
- Hassaan ibn Thaabit (RA)
- Hamnah bint Jahsh (RA)

Incident of Slander

he Prophet ﷺ himself was unsure of what had taken place until Allah SWT revealed verses in her defense:

إِلَّا الَّذِينَ تَابُوا مِنْ بَعْدِ ذٰلِكَ وَ أَصْلَحُوا فَإِنَّ اللّٰهَ غَفُورٌ رَّحِيمٌ ﴿٥﴾ وَ الَّذِينَ يَرْمُونَ أَزْوَاجَهُمْ وَ لَمْ يَكُنْ
لَّهُمْ شُهَدَاءُ إِلَّا أَنْفُسُهُمْ فَشَهَادَةُ أَحَدِهِمْ أَرْبَعُ شَهٰدٰتٍ بِاللّٰهِ إِنَّهُ لَمِنَ الصّٰدِقِينَ ﴿٦﴾ وَ الْخَامِسَةُ أَنَّ لَعْنَتَ
اللّٰهِ عَلَيْهِ إِنْ كَانَ مِنَ الْكٰذِبِينَ ﴿٧﴾ وَ يَدْرَؤُا عَنْهَا الْعَذَابَ أَنْ تَشْهَدَ أَرْبَعَ شَهٰدٰتٍ بِاللّٰهِ إِنَّهُ لَمِنَ
الْكٰذِبِينَ ﴿٨﴾ وَ الْخَامِسَةَ أَنَّ غَضَبَ اللّٰهِ عَلَيْهَا إِنْ كَانَ مِنَ الصّٰدِقِينَ ﴿٩﴾ وَ لَوْ لَا فَضْلُ اللّٰهِ عَلَيْكُمْ وَ
رَحْمَتُهُ وَ أَنَّ اللّٰهَ تَوَّابٌ حَكِيمٌ ﴿١٠﴾ إِنَّ الَّذِينَ جَاءُوْ بِالْإِفْكِ عُصْبَةٌ مِّنْكُمْ لَا تَحْسَبُوهُ شَرًّا لَّكُمْ بَلْ هُوَ
خَيْرٌ لَّكُمْ لِكُلِّ امْرِئٍ مِّنْهُمْ مَّا اكْتَسَبَ مِنَ الْإِثْمِ وَ الَّذِي تَوَلّٰى كِبْرَهُ مِنْهُمْ لَهُ عَذَابٌ عَظِيمٌ ﴿١١﴾ لَوْ لَا
إِذْ سَمِعْتُمُوهُ ظَنَّ الْمُؤْمِنُونَ وَ الْمُؤْمِنٰتُ بِأَنْفُسِهِمْ خَيْرًا وَ قَالُوا هٰذَا إِفْكٌ مُّبِينٌ ﴿١٢﴾ لَوْ لَا جَاءُوْ عَلَيْهِ
بِأَرْبَعَةِ شُهَدَاءَ فَإِذْ لَمْ يَأْتُوا بِالشُّهَدَاءِ فَأُولٰئِكَ عِنْدَ اللّٰهِ هُمُ الْكٰذِبُونَ ﴿١٣﴾ وَ لَوْ لَا فَضْلُ اللّٰهِ عَلَيْكُمْ وَ
رَحْمَتُهُ فِي الدُّنْيَا وَ الْآخِرَةِ لَمَسَّكُمْ فِي مَا أَفَضْتُمْ فِيهِ عَذَابٌ عَظِيمٌ ﴿١٤﴾ إِذْ تَلَقَّوْنَهُ بِأَلْسِنَتِكُمْ وَ تَقُولُونَ
بِأَفْوَاهِكُمْ مَّا لَيْسَ لَكُمْ بِهِ عِلْمٌ وَّ تَحْسَبُونَهُ هَيِّنًا وَّ هُوَ عِنْدَ اللّٰهِ عَظِيمٌ ﴿١٥﴾ وَ لَوْ لَا إِذْ سَمِعْتُمُوهُ قُلْتُمْ
مَّا يَكُونُ لَنَا أَنْ نَّتَكَلَّمَ بِهٰذَا سُبْحٰنَكَ هٰذَا بُهْتَانٌ عَظِيمٌ ﴿١٦﴾ يَعِظُكُمُ اللّٰهُ أَنْ تَعُودُوا لِمِثْلِهِ أَبَدًا إِنْ كُنْتُمْ
مُّؤْمِنِينَ ﴿١٧﴾ وَ يُبَيِّنُ اللّٰهُ لَكُمُ الْاٰيٰتِ وَ اللّٰهُ عَلِيمٌ حَكِيمٌ ﴿١٨﴾ إِنَّ الَّذِينَ يُحِبُّونَ أَنْ تَشِيعَ الْفَاحِشَةُ
فِي الَّذِينَ اٰمَنُوا لَهُمْ عَذَابٌ أَلِيمٌ فِي الدُّنْيَا وَ الْاٰخِرَةِ وَ اللّٰهُ يَعْلَمُ وَ أَنْتُمْ لَا تَعْلَمُونَ ﴿١٩﴾ وَ لَوْ لَا فَضْلُ اللّٰهِ
عَلَيْكُمْ وَ رَحْمَتُهُ وَ أَنَّ اللّٰهَ رَءُوفٌ رَّحِيمٌ ﴿٢٠﴾

Unless they repent thereafter and mend (their conduct); for Allah is Oft- Forgiving, Most Merciful(5) And for those who launch a charge against their spouses, and have (in support) no evidence but their own,- their solitary evidence (can be received) if they bear witness four times (with an oath) by Allah that they are solemnly telling the truth(6) And the fifth (oath) (should be) that they solemnly invoke the curse of Allah on themselves if they tell a lie(7) But it would avert the punishment from the wife, if she bears witness four times (with an oath) By Allah, that (her husband) is telling a lie(8) And the fifth (oath) should be that she solemnly invokes the wrath of Allah on herself if (her accuser) is telling the truth(9) If it were not for Allah's grace and mercy on you, and that Allah is Oft- Returning, full of Wisdom,- (Ye would be ruined indeed)(10) Those who brought forward the lie are a body among yourselves: think it not to be an evil to you; On the contrary it is good for you: to every man among them (will come the punishment) of the sin that he earned, and to him who took on himself the lead among them, will be a penalty grievous(11) Why did not the believers - men and women - when ye heard of the affair,- put the best construction on it in their own minds and say, "This (charge) is an obvious lie" ?(12) Why did they not bring four witnesses to prove it? When they have not brought the witnesses, such men, in the sight of Allah, (stand forth) themselves as liars!(13) Were it not for the grace and mercy of Allah on you, in this world and the Hereafter, a grievous penalty would have seized you in that ye rushed glibly into this affair(14) Behold, ye received it on your tongues, and said out of your mouths things of which ye had no knowledge; and ye thought it to be a light matter, while it was most serious in the sight of Allah(15) And why did ye not, when ye heard it, say? - "It is not right of us to speak of this: Glory to Allah. this is a most serious slander!"(16) Allah doth admonish you, that ye may never repeat such (conduct), if ye are (true) Believers(17) And Allah makes the Signs plain to you: for Allah is full of knowledge and wisdom(18) Those who love (to see) scandal published broadcast among the Believers, will have a grievous Penalty in this life and in the Hereafter: Allah knows, and ye know not(19) Were it not for the grace and mercy of Allah on you, and that Allah is full of kindness and mercy, (ye would be ruined indeed).(20)[24:5-20]

Battle of Khandaq

Causes for the Battle of Khandaq:

- A group of Jews from Banu Nadheer went to Mecca and encouraged the Quraysh to mount an attack against the Muslims
- The Quraysh called upon their allies and gathered an army of 10,000

Salman Al-Farisi

- Khandaq: "Trench"

Miracles During Khandaq

pon completing the trench, the Muslims prepared 3,000 men for battle.

li (RA) vs. ‘Amr ibn ‘Abd -Wud

rophet Muhammad’s ﷺ Du’a

The Hypocrites & Believers in Surah Al-Ahzab:

وَ اِذْ قَالَتْ طَّآئِفَةٌ مِّنْهُمْ يٰۤاَهْلَ يَثْرِبَ لَا مُقَامَ لَكُمْ فَارْجِعُوْا ۚ وَ يَسْتَاْذِنُ فَرِيْقٌ مِّنْهُمُ النَّبِىَّ
يَقُوْلُوْنَ اِنَّ بُيُوْتَنَا عَوْرَةٌ ۛ وَ مَا هِىَ بِعَوْرَةٍ ۚ اِنْ يُّرِيْدُوْنَ اِلَّا فِرَارًا ﴿۱۳﴾

And when a faction of them said, “ O people of Yathrib, there is no stability for you [here], so return [home].” And a party of them asked permission of the Prophet, saying, “Indeed, our houses are unprotected,” while they were not exposed. They did not intend except to flee. [33:13]

وَ لَمَّا رَاَ الْمُؤْمِنُوْنَ الْاَحْزَابَ ۙ قَالُوْا هٰذَا مَا وَعَدَنَا اللّٰهُ وَ رَسُوْلُهٗ وَ صَدَقَ اللّٰهُ وَ رَسُوْلُهٗ ۫
وَ مَا زَادَهُمْ اِلَّاۤ اِيْمَانًا وَّ تَسْلِيْمًا ﴿۲۲﴾

And when the believers saw the companies, they said, “This is what Allah SWT and His Messenger had promised us, and Allah SWT and His Messenger spoke the truth.” And it increased them only in faith and acceptance. [33:22]

The Expulsion of Banu Quraydha

Violation of the Treaty:

- During the Battle of Khandaq, Banu Quraydha were convinced to break their treaty with the Prophet ﷺ
- The Muslims had just returned to Madinah from the battle when Jibreel came with the command to attack Banu Quraydha
- The Prophet ﷺ commanded them to set out immediately and told them not pray Asr until they reach Banu Quraydha

Muslim Besiege Banu Quraydha for Nearly a Month

- Abu Lubabah is sent to mediate and his blunder

The Decision of Sa'd ibn Mu'ath (RA)

The Prophet ﷺ said: *"You have ruled with that which Allah SWT decreed from above the seven skies."*

Allah's SWT Throne Shakes

Events After the Expulsion

The Prophet's ﷺ marriage to Zaynab bint Jahsh (RA)

The Islam of Thumamah ibn Uthaal (RA)

Avenging the Martyrs of Raji'

Year of Expeditions

Expedition of Muhammad ibn Maslamah

Expedition of Abu 'Ubaidah ibn Al-Jarrah

Expedition of Tarif

Expedition of Hasma

Expedition of Dawmat-ul-Jandal

Expedition of Kurz ibn Jaabir Fihri

Expedition of Amr ibn Umayyah Dhamri

The Prophet's ﷺ Advice

- Before the expedition of Dawmat-ul-Jandal, some young Ansar asked the Prophet ﷺ :

  Who is the best Muslim? Who is the most intelligent?

- The Prophet ﷺ answered and then advised them to stay away from five evil practices

Phase Review Questions

1. What was the name of Abu Bakr's (RA) eldest daughter?

2. Who came to give the report to Abu Bakr (RA) while he was in the cave?

3. Who would come feed the Prophet ﷺ ?

4. What were the two miracles that happened while Abu Bakr (RA) and the Prophet ﷺ were in the cave?

5. What was the Prophecy regarding Suraqah ibn Malik (RA)?

6. How long did the Prophet ﷺ stay in Quba?

7. Why did the calendar not start on the Prophet ﷺ birthday?

8. When was the Islamic Calendar officially established?

9. Where did the first Jummah take place?

Phase Review Questions

10. What were the main topics?

11. Why did the Jews initially settle in Madinah?

12. How did the Jews react when the Prophet ﷺ entered Madinah?

13. Where did Salman Al-Farisi come from? What religion did they practice there?

14. Who built the home of Abu Ayyub?

15. What was the purpose of forming brotherhoods?

16. What were the two main tribes of Madinah and who were their leaders?

17. Why were Ansar given that name?

18. Why did the companions struggle to acclimate to Madinah?

Phase Review Questions

19. What was the original size of the Masjid in Madinah?

20. Who saw the dream of the Athan?

21. What were the three main Jewish tribes?

22. Who purchased the well of Ruma?

23. What is one virtue of 'Aisha (RA)?

24. What was the initial Qiblah?

25. How long after Hijrah did it change?

26. Why did the Qiblah change?

27. Who are Ashaab Al-Suffa? Who is the most famous among them?

Phase Review Questions

28. What is the difference between a Ghazwa and a Sariyya?

29. How many Ghazwas and Sariyyas took place?

30. How many Ghazwas had physical combat?

31. Who was the first to fire an arrow in Islam?

32. What caused the Battle of Badr? When did it take place?

33. How many Muslims attended the battle? How many Non-Muslims?

34. Who carried the main flag of the Muslims?

35. How many angels were sent down in aid of the Muslims?

36. Who killed Abu Jahl?

Phase Review Questions

37. How many Muslims were killed?

38. Where was 'Uthman (RA) during this battle?

39. What is one lesson you can derive from this battle?

40. What was the reaction of the Quraysh after the battle?

41. What marriage took place after this battle?

42. Why was Ka'b ibn Al-Ashraf assassinated?

43. Which Jewish tribe was expelled and why?

44. What caused the battle of Uhud?

45. Who warned the Prophet ﷺ about the plot?

Phase Review Questions

46. How many Muslims attended this battle? How many Non-Muslims?

47. What was the mistake of the archers? What did this cause?

48. Who killed Hamza (RA)?

49. What is the main lesson from Uhud?

50. Why did the ten companions go out to Raji'?

51. How many companions were killed at Bir Ma'oonah?

52. Why did the Muslims attack Banu Nadheer?

53. What is one wisdom of alcohol being prohibited in stages?

54. Why did Thaatur Riqa' take place?

Phase Review Questions

55. What does Riqa' mean? Why was it named this?

56. Why did the hypocrites attend Banu Al-Mustaliq?

57. Why was 'Aisha (RA) delayed from the caravan?

58. How was her innocence proven?

59. What was the goal of the non-Muslims in Khandaq?

60. How many non-Muslims were gathered?

61. Who suggested the digging of the trench?

62. How were the non-Muslims defeated?

63. Why did the battle of Banu Quraydha take place?

64. What happened at the death of Sa'd ibn Mu'ath?

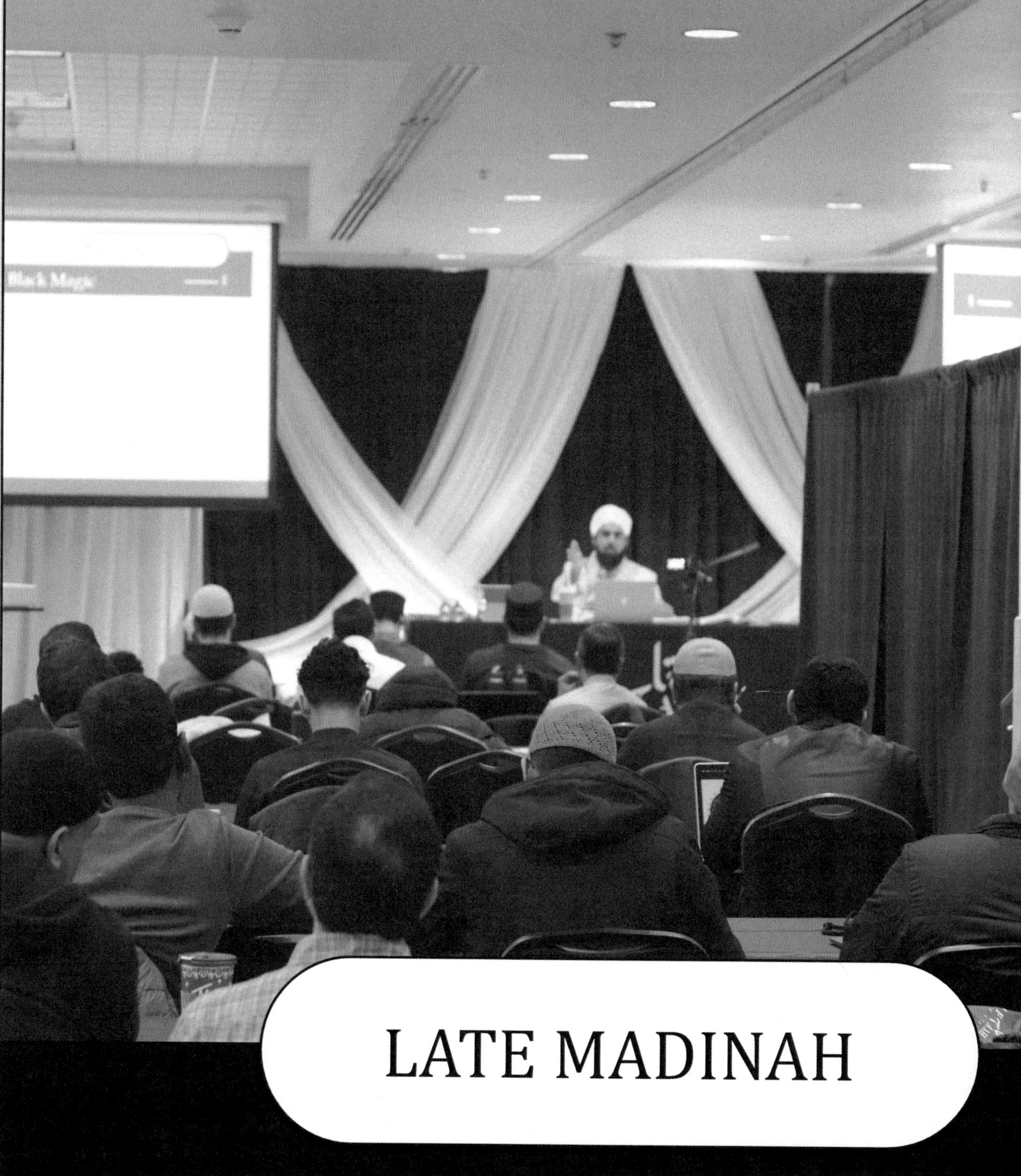

LATE MADINAH

A period in which the Muslims had established themselves and faced constant threats. Islam is able to spread massively in this period, and the Muslims become a superpower. The death of the Prophet ﷺ came shortly after Islam's dominance.

LATE MADINAH

- Prophethood Map
- Hudaybiyya
- Treaty of Hudaybiyya
- The Year of Delegations
- Black Magic
- Battle in Khaybar
- Aftermath of Khaybar
- Wadi Al-Qura’
- ‘Umratul Qada’
- Death of Zaynab bint Muhammad (RA)
- Khalid ibn Al-Waleed (RA) and ‘Amr ibn Al’Aas (RA)
- Construction of the Pulpit
- Battle of Muta
- Dhaat us-Salaasil
- Saif ul-Bahr
- Conquest of Mecca
- Battle of Hunayn
- Siege of Ta’if

LATE MADINAH

- Aftermath of Hunayn
- Expedition of Tabuk
- Between Tabuk and the Farwell Pilgrimage
- Farewell Pilgrimage
- Ghadir Khum
- Army of Usama ibn Zayd
- Indications of the Prophet's ﷺ Death
- Fatal Illness
- The Last Sermon
- The Last Prayer
- The Passing of the Prophet ﷺ
- The Reactions of the Companions
- Phase Review Questions

Prophethood Map

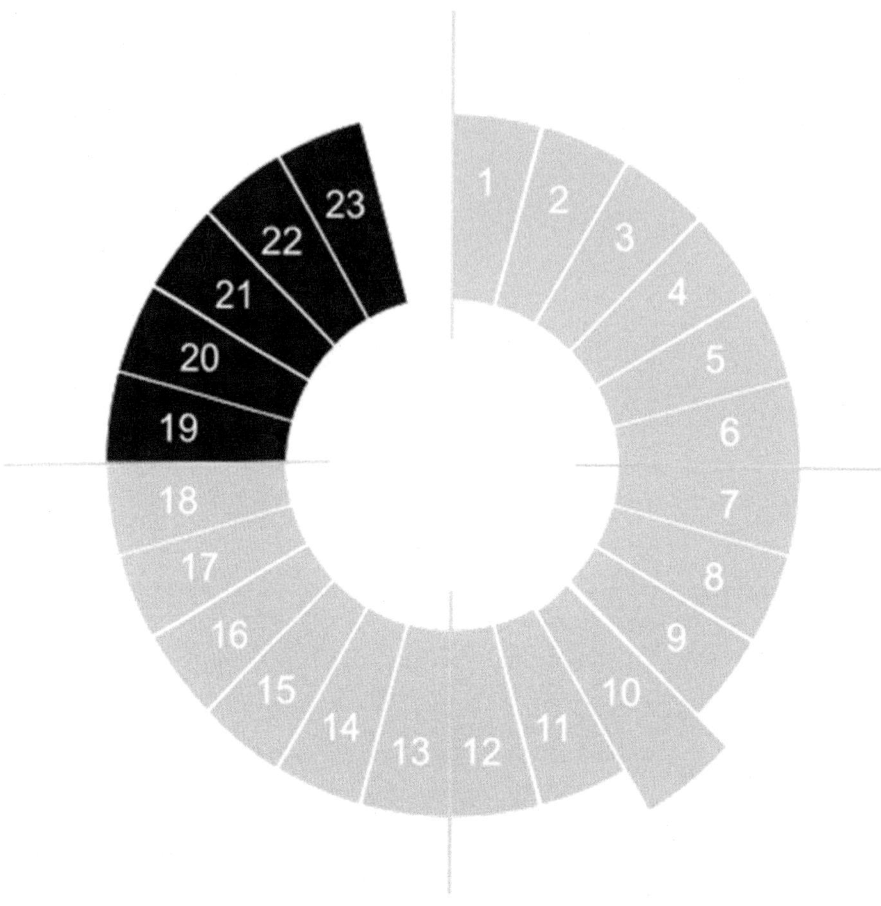

Hudaybiyya
The Muslims sign a peace treaty that ends hostilities with the Meccans

Umrah
The Muslims perform the Umrah they were prevented from in the previous year

Conquest of Mecca
10,000 Muslims enter and peacefully reclaim Mecca

Tabuk
The largest Muslim army ever assembled headed out to confront the Romans at Tabuk

Farewell Pilgrimage
The Prophet ﷺ performs his only Hajj and leads over 100,000 Muslims

Hudaybiyya

In the month of Dhul-qa'dah, six years after the Hijrah, the Prophet ﷺ witnesses a dream instructing him to make Umrah.

A caravan of 1,000-1,500 pilgrims headed towards Mecca unarmed, wearing Ihram.

Khalid ibn Waleed attempts to intercept the caravan

- Miracle of water from the fingers of the Prophet ﷺ

The Meccans prevented the Muslims from entering Mecca, and then sent multiple negotiators to attempt to reach agreement.

- 'Urwah ibn Mas'ood

'Uthman (RA)

Bay'aat-ur-Ridwaan

Treaty of Hudaybiyya

Terms:

- 10 years of peace
- Meccans seeking refuge in Madinah will have to be returned to Mecca, but Madinans moving to Mecca will remain
- The Muslims will return to Madinah for Umrah the next year but can only remain in Mecca for three days
- Any tribe wanting to ally with the Muslims or the Quraysh can do so (Banu Khuza'a and Banu Bakr)

Story of Abu Jandal

Reaction of the Companions

- Advice of Umm Salamah (RA)

- Umar (RA)

Surah Al-Fath

Year of Delegations

udaybiyya paved the way for the year of delegations to take place.

he most notable delegations:

- Arabian tribes of Hawazin and Thaqeef, Daws, the Ash'ariyyin, and Najran
- The emperor of Rome, Persia, Abyssinia, and Egypt

In the name of God, the Gracious One, the Merciful. From Muhammad, servant of God and His messenger to Heraclius, leader of the Romans:

Peace unto whoever follows the guided path! Thereafter, I call you to submit your will to God. Submit your will to God and you will be safe. God shall compensate your reward two-folds. But if you turn away, then you will bear the sin of your followers. Then "O people of the Book, come to a word common between us and you, that we worship none but Allah, that we associate nothing with Him and that some of us do not take others as Lords instead of Allah. Then, should they turn back, say: bear witness that we are Muslim" [Quran 3:64]

Seal: Muhammad, Messenger of God

Abu Sufyan and Heraclius

- Among what Abu Sufyan said was:

"He commands us to worship Allah SWT and to abstain from ascribing any partners unto Him. He commanded us to immediately forsake all our ancestral customs of shirk and kufr perpetrated by our forefathers. He also instructs us to perform Salaah and pay Zakat and to adhere to truthfulness, chastity, and favorable family ties".

Black Magic

Before Khaybar, black magic was done on the Prophet ﷺ

- The people of Khaybar called upon their most renowned sorcerer named Labid

- The effect of Black Magic on the Prophet ﷺ

- The revelation of Surah Al-Falaq and Surah Al-Naas

بِسۡمِ اللّٰهِ الرَّحۡمٰنِ الرَّحِيۡمِ

قُلۡ اَعُوۡذُ بِرَبِّ الۡفَلَقِ ﴿۱﴾ مِنۡ شَرِّ مَا خَلَقَ ﴿۲﴾ وَ مِنۡ شَرِّ غَاسِقٍ اِذَا وَقَبَ ﴿۳﴾ وَ
مِنۡ شَرِّ النَّفّٰثٰتِ فِی الۡعُقَدِ ﴿۴﴾
وَ مِنۡ شَرِّ حَاسِدٍ اِذَا حَسَدَ ٪﴿۵﴾

Say: I seek refuge with the Lord of the Dawn (1) From the mischief of created things (2) From the mischief of Darkness as it overspreads (3) From the mischief of those who practice secret arts (4) And from the mischief of the envious one as he practices envy (5)[113:1-5]

بِسۡمِ اللّٰهِ الرَّحۡمٰنِ الرَّحِيۡمِ

قُلۡ اَعُوۡذُ بِرَبِّ النَّاسِ ﴿۱﴾ مَلِکِ النَّاسِ ﴿۲﴾ اِلٰهِ النَّاسِ ﴿۳﴾ مِنۡ شَرِّ الۡوَسۡوَاسِ
الۡخَنَّاسِ ﴿۴﴾ الَّذِیۡ یُوَسۡوِسُ فِیۡ صُدُوۡرِ النَّاسِ ﴿۵﴾ مِنَ الۡجِنَّةِ وَ النَّاسِ ﴿۶﴾

Say: I seek refuge with the Lord and Cherisher of Mankind (1) The King (or Ruler) of Mankind (2) The Allah (for judge) of Mankind (3) From the mischief of the Whisperer (of Evil), who withdraws (after his whisper) (4) (The same) who whispers into the hearts of Mankind (5) Among Jinn and among men (6) [114:1-6]

Effects of the Evil Eye

Battle in Khaybar

لَقَدْ رَضِيَ اللّٰهُ عَنِ الْمُؤْمِنِيْنَ اِذْ يُبَايِعُوْنَكَ تَحْتَ الشَّجَرَةِ فَعَلِمَ مَا فِيْ قُلُوْبِهِمْ فَاَنْزَلَ السَّكِيْنَةَ عَلَيْهِمْ وَ اَثَابَهُمْ فَتْحًا قَرِيْبًا ﴿١٨﴾

Certainly was Allah SWT pleased with the believers when they pledged allegiance to you, [O Muhammad], under the tree, and He knew what was in their hearts, so He sent down tranquility upon them and rewarded them with an imminent conquest (48:18)

وَّ مَغَانِمَ كَثِيْرَةً يَّاْخُذُوْنَهَا ؕ وَ كَانَ اللّٰهُ عَزِيْزًا حَكِيْمًا ﴿١٩﴾

And much war booty which they will take. And ever is Allah SWT Exalted in Might and Wise. (48:19)

The battle of Khaybar took place immediately after Hudaybiyya

- Hypocrites were not allowed to join the battle

Cause of the Battle

- They broke the treaty with the Muslims many times
    - Encouraged the non-Muslims to gather in the battle of the trench
    - Encouraged Banu Quraydha to break their treaty with the Muslims

The Muslims marched forth to Khaybar, just outside of Madinah, with 1,400 companions on foot and 200 on rides (horses/camels).

- Jews were not surprised, Abdullah ibn Ubayy warned them about the raid
- They received aid from surrounding tribes and had a total of 14,000 men defending the fortresses

Battle in Khaybar

- Aamir ibn Awka recited a poem, when the Prophet ﷺ heard he said: “May Allah SWT have mercy on him”
  - This was an indication that he would be martyred

The Five Main Forts of Khaybar

- Naim
- Qamus
- Saab ibn Muaz
- Qullah
- Watih and Salalim

Ali and Marhab

Ali (RA) in Khaybar

Battle in Khaybar

The Siege of Khaybar

The Prophet ﷺ Gets Poisoned

Aftermath of Khaybar

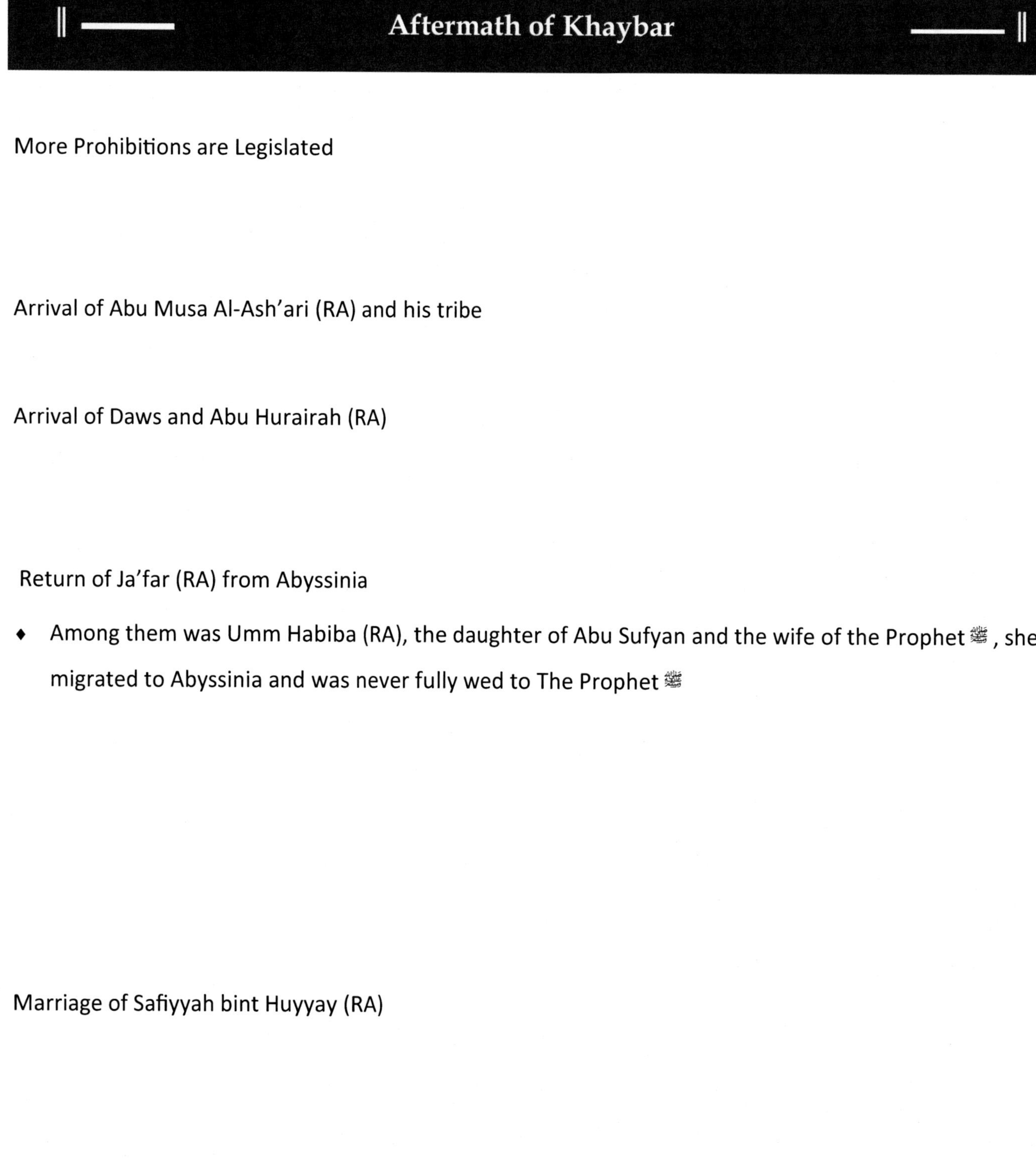

More Prohibitions are Legislated

Arrival of Abu Musa Al-Ash'ari (RA) and his tribe

Arrival of Daws and Abu Hurairah (RA)

Return of Ja'far (RA) from Abyssinia

- Among them was Umm Habiba (RA), the daughter of Abu Sufyan and the wife of the Prophet ﷺ, she migrated to Abyssinia and was never fully wed to The Prophet ﷺ

Marriage of Safiyyah bint Huyyay (RA)

Wadi Al-Qura

59

Wadi Al-Qura and the Jews

'Amr ibn Sa'eed ibn Al-'Aas (RA) leads the expedition

'Umratul Qada'

The Prophet ﷺ and his companions return to perform the 'Umrah they were denied in Hudaybiyya 60

- 2,000 Muslims perform Umrah

7

Death of Zaynab bint Muhammad (RA)

61

he eldest daughter of Prophet Muhammad's ﷺ demise

She died from a wound inflicted by Habbar ibn Aswad during her migration.

She passed away in the year 8 A.H.

Khalid ibn al-Waleed (RA) and 'Amr ibn al'Aas (RA)

Khalid ibn al-Waleed (RA)

Amr ibn al'Aas (RA)

'Uthman ibn Talha (RA)

Construction of the Pulpit

A woman from the Ansar suggests that a pulpit is built for the Prophet ﷺ

The pulpit consisted of three steps and a small platform

It was initially built next to a tree trunk which the Prophet ﷺ would lean on

The Tree Trunk

Battle of Muta

This battle took place because Haaris ibn 'Umair was intercepted and killed by Shurahbeel ibn 'Amr from Ghassan on the way to the Roman emperor.

- The Muslims came with 3,000 men while the non-Muslims had amassed 100,000 soldiers
- The Prophet ﷺ appointed a chain of command consisting of Zaid ibn Haritha (RA), Ja'far ibn Abu Talib (RA), and Abdullah ibn Rawaha (RA)

- Abdullah ibn Rawaha

- Khalid ibn Waleed's (RA) first battle as a Muslim

Battle of Muta

he 12 Martyrs

- Zaid ibn Harithah (RA)
- Ja'far ibn Abu Talib (RA)
- 'Abdullah ibn Rawaahah (RA)
- Mas'ood ibn Aws (RA)
- Wahab ibn S'ad (RA)
- Haaris ibn Nu'maan (RA)
- Suraaqah ibn Umar (RA)
- 'Abbaad ibn Qays (RA)
- Abu Kulaib ibn 'Amr (RA)
- Jaabir ibn 'Amr (RA)
- 'Amr ibn S'ad ibn Haaris (RA)
- Amer ibn S'ad (RA)

Dhaat us Salaasil

An expedition takes place in Jamadul-Akhir.

'Amr ibn Al-'Aas (RA), a new Muslim, led the expedition.

The Muslims set out with 500 men in total to confront Banu Quda'ah.

Muslims are Victorious

Saif ul-Bahr

xpedition near the coastal areas of Hijaz

ed by Abu 'Ubaidah (RA)

Battle of Khabt

- Khabt meaning dry leaves

- They found a large sea creature which they ate from

The Conquest of Mecca

The Violation of the Treaty of Hudaybiyya

- Men from the tribe of Banu Bakr, an ally of the Quryash attacked Banu Khuza'ah, a Muslim ally
- The Prophet ﷺ attempted to reconcile and maintain the Treaty of Hudaybiyya, but the Quraysh refused
- Abu Sufyan came to Madinah in an attempt to ask the Muslims for forgiveness, but he was ignored by the people of Madinah

Hatim ibn Abi Balta'ah sent a letter to Quraysh informing them of the Muslims' plan.

The Muslims depart from Madinah with approximately 10,000 people.

The Prophet ﷺ visits his mother's grave.

The Conquest of Mecca

he Last Muhajir

Muslims On Route to Mecca

The Muslims Camp Outside of Mecca

Abu Sufyan ibn Harb (RA) and Abu Sufyan ibn Al-Harith (RA) Accept Islam

- Zubair (RA) was carrying the flag of Muhajireen
- Sa'd ibn 'Ubadah (RA) was carrying flag of Ansar
    - He was chanting: "Today is the day of the massacre"
    - The Prophet ﷺ said: *"Sa'd has lied, today is the day of mercy"*

Abu Sufyan ibn Harb's (RA) Reaction to Sa'd ibn 'Ubadah (RA)

The Conquest of Mecca

The Prophet's ﷺ Entry into Mecca

The Difference between a King and a Prophet

Keys of the Ka'bah

The Prophet ﷺ Pardons the Meccans

Bilal (RA) Gives the Athan on the Ka'ba

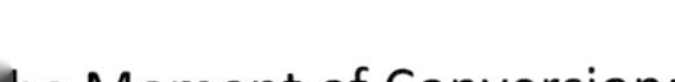

The Conquest of Mecca

he Moment of Conversion:

'Ikramah ibn Abi Jahl (Fled initially then returned)

Hind bint 'Utbah (the wife of Abu Sufyan)

- Safwan ibn Umayyah

- Harith ibn Hisham

- Habbar ibn al-Aswad

- Abu Quhafah

- Fudalah

The Battle of Hunayn

لَقَدْ نَصَرَكُمُ اللّٰهُ فِيْ مَوَاطِنَ كَثِيْرَةٍ ۙ وَّ يَوْمَ حُنَيْنٍ ۙ اِذْ اَعْجَبَتْكُمْ كَثْرَتُكُمْ فَلَمْ تُغْنِ عَنْكُمْ
شَيْـًٔا وَّ ضَاقَتْ عَلَيْكُمُ الْاَرْضُ بِمَا رَحُبَتْ ثُمَّ وَلَّيْتُمْ مُّدْبِرِيْنَ ﴿۲۵﴾ ثُمَّ اَنْزَلَ اللّٰهُ سَكِيْنَتَهٗ
عَلٰى رَسُوْلِهٖ وَ عَلَى الْمُؤْمِنِيْنَ وَ اَنْزَلَ جُنُوْدًا لَّمْ تَرَوْهَا وَ عَذَّبَ الَّذِيْنَ كَفَرُوْا ؕ وَ ذٰلِكَ جَزَآءُ
الْكٰفِرِيْنَ ﴿۲۶﴾ ثُمَّ يَتُوْبُ اللّٰهُ مِنْۢ بَعْدِ ذٰلِكَ عَلٰى مَنْ يَّشَآءُ ؕ وَ اللّٰهُ غَفُوْرٌ رَّحِيْمٌ
﴿۲۷﴾

Assuredly Allah did help you in many battle-fields and on the day of Hunain: Behold! your great numbers elated you, but they availed you naught: the land, for all that it is wide, did constrain you, and ye turned back in retreat (25) But Allah did pour His calm on the Messenger and on the Believers, and sent down forces which ye saw not: He punished the Unbelievers; thus doth He reward those without Faith (26) Again will Allah, after this, turn (in mercy) to whom He will: for Allah is Oft-forgiving, Most Merciful (27) [9:25-27]

The Largest Muslim Army to Date

- 12,000 Muslims vs. 20,000 non-Muslims

This battle took place because the tribe of Hawazin and the tribe of Banu Thaqeef planned to attack the Muslims.

Commencement of the Battle

Muslims on their Heels

Angels Descend in Aid of the Muslims

Shaybah ibn 'Uthman ibn Abi Talha

The Siege of Ta'if

ome of the defeated armies of Hunayn fled to Ta'if and took shelter in a fortress.

Muslims Besiege the Fortress

The Prophet ﷺ made du'a for the the Tribe of Thaqeef's guidance.

The Aftermath of Hunayn

Distribution of the Spoils of War

The Reaction of the Ansar

The Foster Sister of the Prophet ﷺ

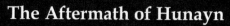

The Second Umrah

The Expedition of Tabuk

he final expedition of the Prophet ﷺ

he Cause:

The Roman Empire amassed 100,000 soldiers

'his was a time of extreme heat, drought, and financial struggle.

\ll Eligible Muslims Obligated to Participate

/erses of Surah Tawba

The Prophet ﷺ encouraged the companions to give full support.

'Uthman (RA)

Abu Bakr (RA) and Umar (RA)

Abdulrahman ibn 'Awf (RA)

The poor companions desired to participate.

9

The Expedition of Tabuk

The Muslim army was composed of 30,000 soldiers.

Ali ibn Abi Talib (RA) was placed in charge of Madinah.

The Journey to Tabuk

- Abu Dharr (RA)

- The Prophet ﷺ prayed Fajr behind Abdul Rahman ibn ‘Awf (RA)

- Drinking from the River of Tabuk

The Prophet ﷺ reached Tabuk and spent 20 days awaiting the Roman army

- No army came to fight the Muslims
- Treaties made with nearby tribes

The Expedition of Tabuk

he Muslims Return to Madinah

Excuses of the Munafiqeen

There were three companions that did not participate:

- Ka'ab ibn Malik
- Murarah ibn Al-Rabee',
- Hilal ibn Umayyah

The Social Boycott

وَّ عَلَى الثَّلٰثَةِ الَّذِيْنَ خُلِّفُوْا۔حَتّٰۤى اِذَا ضَاقَتْ عَلَيْهِمُ الْاَرْضُ بِمَا رَحُبَتْ وَ ضَاقَتْ عَلَيْهِمْ اَنْفُسُهُمْ وَ ظَنُّوْۤا اَنْ لَّا مَلْجَاَ مِنَ اللّٰهِ اِلَّاۤ اِلَيْهِ۔ثُمَّ تَابَ عَلَيْهِمْ لِيَتُوْبُوْا۔اِنَّ اللّٰهَ هُوَ التَّوَّابُ الرَّحِيْمُ ﴿۱۱۸﴾

(He turned in mercy also) to the three who were left behind; (they felt guilty) to such a degree that the earth seemed constrained to them, for all its spaciousness, and their (very) souls seemed straitened to them,- and they perceived that there is no fleeing from Allah (and no refuge) but to Himself. Then He turned to them, that they might repent: for Allah is Oft-Returning, Most Merciful [9:118]

Between Tabuk and the Farewell Pilgrimage

Death of Umm Kulthoom (RA)

Death of Abdullah ibn Ubayy (RA)

Hajj of Abu Bakr (RA)

Mu'ath ibn Jabal (RA) and Abu Musa Al-Ash'ari (RA) are sent to Yemen.

Death of Ibrahim ibn Muhammad (RA)

Ali (RA) and Khalid ibn Al-Waleed (RA) are sent to Yemen

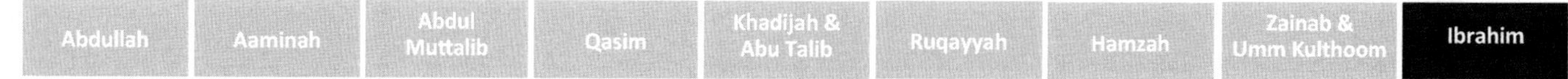

The Farewell Pilgrimage

he Prophet ﷺ Announces Hajj

Muslims gathered from every corner to perform Hajj with the Prophet ﷺ

Between 90,000-114,000 Muslims attended this Hajj

This incident is where scholars gather all of the descriptions of the Hajj of the Prophet ﷺ.

One of the final verses of the Quran was revealed on the day of 'Arafah:

اَلْيَوْمَ يَئِسَ الَّذِيْنَ كَفَرُوْا مِنْ دِيْنِكُمْ فَلَا تَخْشَوْهُمْ وَ اخْشَوْنِ ؕ اَلْيَوْمَ اَكْمَلْتُ لَكُمْ دِيْنَكُمْ وَ
اَتْمَمْتُ عَلَيْكُمْ نِعْمَتِيْ وَ رَضِيْتُ لَكُمُ الْاِسْلَامَ دِيْنًا ؕ فَمَنِ اضْطُرَّ فِيْ مَخْمَصَةٍ غَيْرَ
مُتَجَانِفٍ لِّاِثْمٍ ۙ فَاِنَّ اللّٰهَ غَفُوْرٌ رَّحِيْمٌ ﴿٣﴾

This day have those who reject faith given up all hope of your religion: yet fear them not but fear Me. This day have I perfected your religion for you, completed My favour upon you, and have chosen for you Islam as your religion. But if any is forced by hunger, with no inclination to transgression, Allah is indeed Oft-forgiving, Most Merciful. [5:3]

10

The Farewell Pilgrimage

The Farewell Sermon on the Day of 'Arafa [Sahih Muslim]:

"O people! Listen attentively to what I have to say. It is possible that I will not meet you next year. O people! Your lives, your honor and your wealth are all sacred to each other just as this day, this month, and this city are all sacred. All the matters related to jaahiliyyah are all crushed beneath my feet. All the jahili claims of blood are forgiven. I first of all forgive the Banu Huzayl for the blood of Rabi'ah ibn Haaris ibn 'Abdil Muttalib. All the interest and usury of jaahili times is written off. You may only keep the capital wealth. I first of all write off the usury of 'Abbaas ibn 'Abdul Muttalib." The Prophet ﷺ then explained the mutual rights of husband and wife. "I am leaving behind such a firm thing, that if you hold on to it, you will never go astray: The Book of Allah SWT and the Sunnah of the Prophet ﷺ. On the day of resurrection you will be asked about me. What reply will you give?" The Sahabah replied: "We will testify that you conveyed Allah's SWT message to us, that you fulfilled the trust of Allah SWT and that you desired the well-being of the ummah." The Prophet ﷺ pointed his index finger to the sky and said three times:

اَللّٰهُمَّ اَشْهَد

Main Points of the Sermon

- Justice
- Financial Dealings
- Family Dealings
- Worship
- Equality of all people
- Taqwa
- Conveying the message of Islam to others

Ghadir Khum

ermon delivered by the Prophet ﷺ at the River of Khum, between Mecca and Madinah.

Virtues of the Family of the Prophet ﷺ

Army of Usama ibn Zaid (RA)

Final Expedition Dispatched by the Prophet ﷺ

Date: 26th of Safar

An army of 3000 soldiers was led by Usama ibn Zaid (RA)

Age of Usama ibn Zaid (RA)

Companions Question Usama ibn Zaid's (RA) Leadership

Army is Delayed due to the Prophet ﷺ Sickness

Indications of the Prophet's ﷺ Death

Surah An-Nasr:

بِسۡمِ اللهِ الرَّحۡمٰنِ الرَّحِيۡمِ

اِذَا جَآءَ نَصۡرُ اللّٰهِ وَ الۡفَتۡحُ ﴿۱﴾ وَ رَاَيۡتَ النَّاسَ يَدۡخُلُوۡنَ فِىۡ دِيۡنِ اللّٰهِ اَفۡوَاجًا ﴿۲﴾

فَسَبِّحۡ بِحَمۡدِ رَبِّکَ وَ اسۡتَغۡفِرۡهُ ؕ اِنَّهٗ كَانَ تَوَّابًا ﴿۳﴾

When comes the Help of Allah, and Victory (1) And thou dost see the people enter Allah.s Religion in crowds (2) Celebrate the praises of thy Lord, and pray for His Forgiveness: For He is Oft-Returning (in Grace and Mercy) (3) [110:1-3]

Revision of the Quran

Extended 'Itikaf

Hadith Jibreel

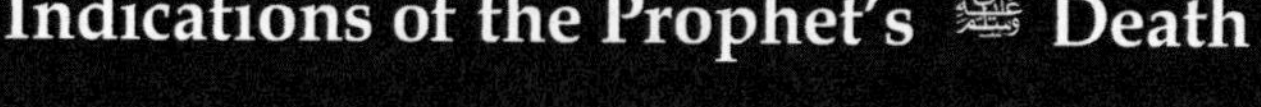

Indications of the Prophet's ﷺ Death

Extensive Worship

Verbal Indication During Hajj:

"I may not meet many of you after this year".

Uhud and Baqi'

Private Conversation with Fatima (RA)

Fatal Illness

ause of Sickness

:arly Signs of Sickness

The Prophet W was nursed in the home of 'Aisha (RA)

Supplications During Sickness

The Last Sermon

The Final Sermon

Choice Between Dunya and Akhira

Virtues of Abu Bakr (RA)

Last Instructions and Advice

The Last Prayer

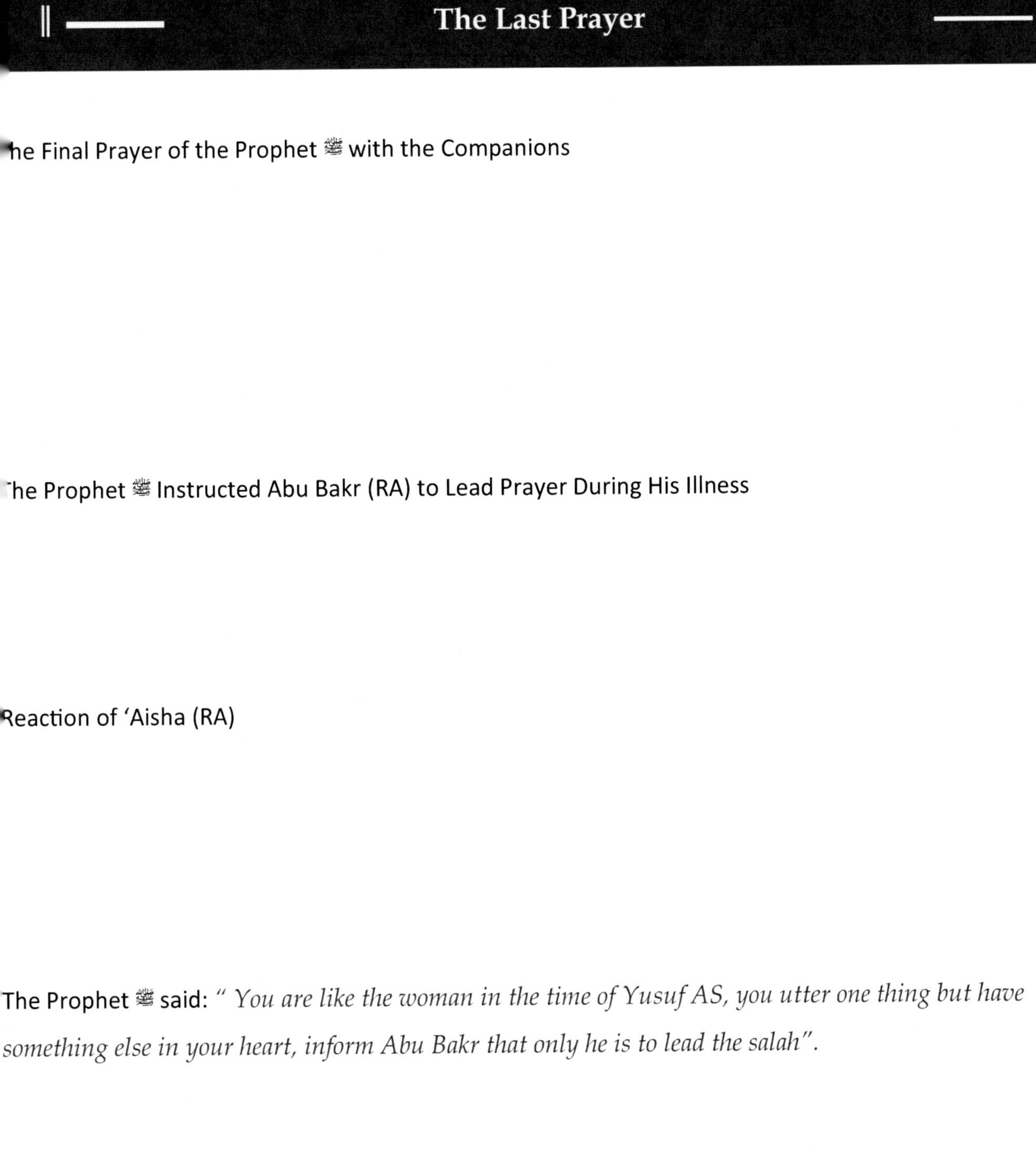

The Final Prayer of the Prophet ﷺ with the Companions

The Prophet ﷺ Instructed Abu Bakr (RA) to Lead Prayer During His Illness

Reaction of ‘Aisha (RA)

The Prophet ﷺ said: *“ You are like the woman in the time of Yusuf AS, you utter one thing but have something else in your heart, inform Abu Bakr that only he is to lead the salah”.*

The Passing of the Prophet ﷺ

63

The Final Glimpse of the Prophet W

The Prophet' s W Health Improves

- Abu Bakr T Takes Permission to Visit Family Outside of Madinah

The Final Moments of the Prophet ﷺ Life

- He constantly repeated the du'a "اللهم الرفيق الاعلى"
  - This means: "Oh Allah SWT, I seek the highest companionship (Jannah)"

Pangs of Death

- He ﷺ returned to Allah SWT in the early afternoon on Monday, the 12th of Rabi' Al-Awwal.
- At the age of 63 and after 23 years of Prophethood

The Reaction of the Companions

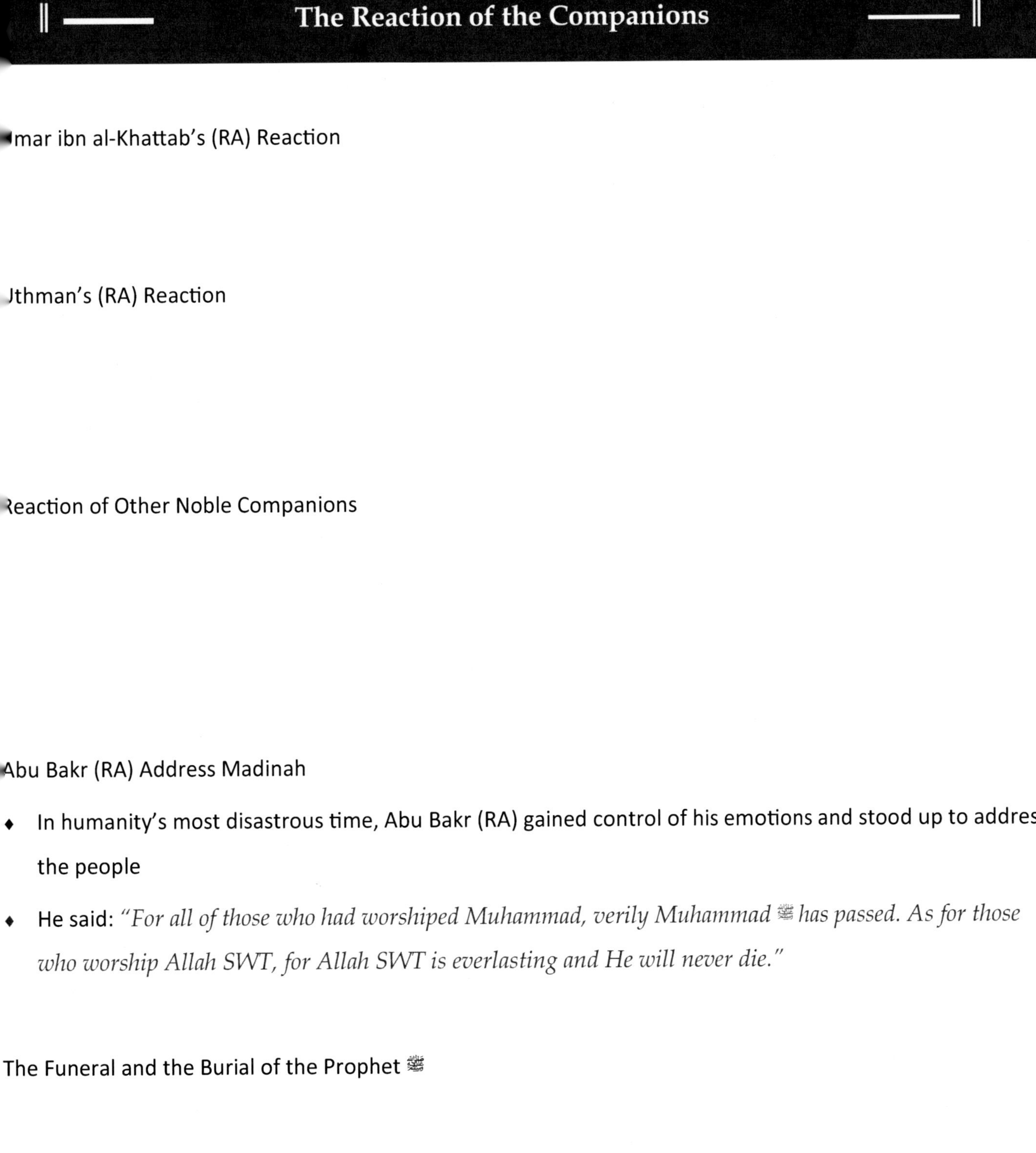

Umar ibn al-Khattab's (RA) Reaction

Uthman's (RA) Reaction

Reaction of Other Noble Companions

Abu Bakr (RA) Address Madinah

- In humanity's most disastrous time, Abu Bakr (RA) gained control of his emotions and stood up to address the people
- He said: *"For all of those who had worshiped Muhammad, verily Muhammad ﷺ has passed. As for those who worship Allah SWT, for Allah SWT is everlasting and He will never die."*

The Funeral and the Burial of the Prophet ﷺ

The Reaction of the Companions

Among the poetry recited in the mourning of the Prophet ﷺ

مَاذَا عَلَيَّ مَنْ شَمَّ تُرْبَةَ أَحْمَدَ ... أَنْ لَّا يَشَمَّ مَدَى الزَّمَانِ غَوَالِيَا
صُبَّتْ عَلَيَّ مَصَائِبُ لَوْ أَنَّهَا ... صُبَّتْ عَلَى الْأَيَّامِ صِرْنَ لَيَالِيَا

The one who has smelt the dirt the Prophet ﷺ lays in, will never experience hardship after this (because every hardship is a blessing compared to this one).

Such calamities have been poured upon me today, that if they were poured upon the days they would turn into nights.

عَنْ أَنَسٍ قَالَ: لَمَّا كَانَ الْيَوْمُ الَّذِي دَخَلَ فِيهِ رَسُولُ اللهِ صَلَّى اللهُ عَلَيْهِ وَسَلَّمَ الْمَدِينَةَ أَضَاءَ مِنْهَا كُلُّ شَيْءٍ، فَلَمَّا كَانَ الْيَوْمُ الَّذِي مَاتَ فِيهِ أَظْلَمَ مِنْهَا كُلُّ شَيْءٍ، وَمَا نَفَضْنَا أَيْدِينَا مِنَ التُّرَابِ، وَإِنَّا لَفِي دَفْنِهِ صَلَّى اللهُ عَلَيْهِ وَسَلَّمَ حَتَّى أَنْكَرْنَا قُلُوبَنَا

Anas ibn Malik (RA) described this incident: *On the day the Prophet ﷺ entered Madinah everything became illuminated, and on the day that he left this world everything became void of light. And we had not yet cleaned our hands after burying him. And we could not complete his burial until we disregarded that which was in our hearts.*

فَجُودِي عَلَيْهِ بِالدُّمُوعِ وَأَعْوِلِي ... لِفَقْدِ الَّذِي لَا مِثْلُهُ الدَّهْرَ يُوجَدُ وَلَا
وَمَا فَقَدَ الْمَاضُونَ مِثْلَ مُحَمَّدٍ ... مِثْلُهُ حَتَّى الْقِيَامَةِ يُفْقَدُ

Hassan ibn Thabit (RA) recited many poems mourning the Prophet ﷺ, among what he said was:

Pour forth with continuous tears, for the loss of the one whom the likes of which will never exist again.

Nor has anyone who has past ever lost anyone similar to Muhammad ﷺ, nor will anyone lose anyone similar to him until the Day of Judgment.

Phase Review Questions

. Why did the Prophet ﷺ lead the companions out to perform Umrah?

. Who was sent to Mecca to negotiate with the Quraysh?

. What caused Bay'at-al-Ridwaan to take place?

. What is one lesson you take from this incident?

. What opportunity arose from Hudaybiyya? What was the result?

. What was the cause of the Battle of Khaybar?

7. How many main fortresses were protecting Khaybar?

8. Which famous companions returned to Madinah after Khaybar?

9. Who had the idea of constructing a pulpit?

Phase Review Questions

10. Who were the Muslims fighting in Muta?

11. Who were the three generals of this army?

12. Who led the expedition of Thaat-us-Salaasil?

13. What does "Khabt" mean?

14. What caused the conquest of Mecca to take place?

15. What was the chant which upset the Prophet ﷺ, who said it, and what did the Prophet ﷺ replace it with?

16. How did the Prophet ﷺ enter into Mecca?

17. How were the Quraysh treated after the years of torment they caused the Muslims?

18. Name three enemies of Islam who converted on this day:

Phase Review Questions

9. What is one lesson you take from this event?

0. What was the cause of this battle?

1. How did Jubair ibn Mut'im describe the descent of the Angels?

2. Who received a large share of the spoils in these battles?

3. What was the cause of Tabuk?

24. Who was commanded to attend this battle?

25. Who were the main companions who funded this battle?

26. How many Muslims fought in this battle?

27. Who were the three individuals who stayed behind without permission?

28. How were they treated and what did Allah SWT mention about them?

Phase Review Questions

29. How many Hajj did the Prophet ﷺ perform in his life?

30. How many people attended the Farewell Pilgrimage?

31. What were some of the main points in the Farewell Sermon?

32. Who did the Prophet ﷺ defend in the incident of Ghadir Khum?

33. How old was Usama ibn Zayd (RA) when he was put in command of an expedition?

34. What was the last complete Surah ever revealed?

35. What were two main points of the Last Sermon?

36. What was the last prayer led by the Prophet ﷺ?

37. On what day did the Prophet ﷺ pass away?

REFERENCES

Al-'Azimi, Musa

Al-Lu'Lu' Al-Maknoon Fi Seeratu Al-Nabi Al-Ma'moon

Ibn Hisham

AbdulMalik. Seeratu Ibn Hisham

Kaandhlawi, *Muhammad Idrees*

Seeratu Al-Mustafa (Abridged Version)

Mohiuddin, Meraj

Revelation: The Story of Muhammad

Mubarakpuri

SafiulRahman. Al-Raheeq Al-Makhtum

وَ اَحْسَنَ مِنْکَ لَمْ تَرَقَطُّ عَیْنِیْ

وَ اَجْمَلَ مِنْکَ لَمْ تَلِدِ النِّسَآءُ

خُلِقْتَ مُبَرَّأً مِّنْ کُلِّ عَیْبٍ

کَاَنَّکَ قَدْ خُلِقْتَ کَمَ تَشَآءُ

More perfect than you my
eyes have never seen.

Nor more beautiful then you a
woman has ever birthed.

You were created free from
any defect.

As if you had been created as
you desire.

@miftaah institute

@miftaah institute

@miftaah.institute

@miftaahinst

@miftaah institute

Made in the USA
Monee, IL
14 December 2022